THE
100 BEST
CURRIES
FOR YOUR INSTANT POT

The Most Delicious, Authentic Indian Recipes Made Easy

HINA GUJRAL

Creator of Fun FOOD Frolic

PAGE STREET
PUBLISHING CO.

PAGE STREET
PUBLISHING CO.

Distributed by Macmillan, sales in Canada by The Canadian Manda Group.

26 25 24 23 22   1 2 3 4 5

ISBN-13: 978-1-64567-540-2

ISBN-10: 1-64567-540-8

Library of Congress Control Number: 2022933869

Cover and book design by Meg Baskis for Page Street Publishing Co.

Photography by Hina Gujral

Printed and bound in the United States of America

Dedicated to my husband Jasmeet for always being
my biggest supporter and critic, and to the memory
of my guardian angel Momo, who will forever
be my guiding star.

❖ CONTENTS ❖

INTRODUCTION

As a child, I was always transfixed by the multitude of curries made daily in our traditional Indian kitchen by the seasoned cooks of the family. The rhythmic stirring of pots, the burst of colors and distinct aromas, a soothing background score of cooking combined with the whistling of a stovetop pressure cooker . . . growing up, I found it all magical and mesmerizing.

In India, food is a ritual and part of our identity. It unifies us and, at the same time, shows the diversity of the nation. From north to south and east to west, food is the common language we all speak and happily share. With this cookbook, I am taking you on a journey of the 100 best curry recipes that you can make easily (and quickly!) at home in an Instant Pot®. Not only are my recipes filled with flavors, but they are also suitable for those who would like to learn how to cook authentic Indian food. A bit of patience and perseverance is the mantra you need to hold while experimenting with Indian food.

It took me 26 years to confess and accept my love for good food. Actually, my flair for cooking came to full bloom after I got married to my soul mate and we set up our first home kitchen in 2010. Ever since, there has been no turning back. I allowed my passion for food to become my purpose and turned it into a profession. Today, I work as a full-time food blogger (yes, that is my bread and butter now), digital creator and social media influencer.

My philosophy is easy, everyday, comfort food—the kind of meals I have grown up eating with my great-grandmother, grandfather, aunts, uncles and cousins. My intercultural marriage into a Sikh family of food lovers, extensive traveling and hours of labor in the kitchen helped me understand the nuances of Indian food in a better way.

Cooking is an art, and it gratifies the people who taste it when we cook with love. And this is the reason that I try to give a personal touch of love to each of my recipe creations. I am sure this cookbook will make you fall in love with Indian flavors.

I am always excited and proud about the variety of ingredients, fresh produce and protein sources we get in India. You will find chapters dedicated to lentil curries, purely vegetarian curries and seafood and meat curries, as well as to the more modern fusion curries and one-pot curried meals.

The word *curry* dates back to when European traders arrived on the shores of India in search of spices. The bright, bold, spicy and soupy Indian dishes with their local names and striking colors were confusing, amusing and intimidating at the same time for travelers and traders. Hence, the term *caril*, or curry, came into existence—a generic word devised by foreign homesteaders to describe the Indian main-course gravy or saucy dishes. And thus began the journey of the word *curry*.

In the past few decades, the upsurge of Indian middle-class nuclear families living away from their homeland required a new style of easy, fast and convenient cooking. As such, the pressure cooker became indispensable in Indian kitchens. The noisy stovetop pressure cooker synced effortlessly with the humdrum of everyday Indian life. The counting of whistles and maintaining the proper stovetop heat were all part of my cooking repertoire until I met the Instant Pot: the Western, more sophisticated cousin of traditional Indian pressure cookers. With the Instant Pot, I felt for the first time that I was in control of the cooking time of my curries. It not only streamlined the cooking process of the dishes but also reintroduced the long-lost concept of slow cooking to my Indian kitchen.

In this cookbook, there is something for every curry lover. Many of the recipes use ingredients readily available outside India, such as kale, butternut squash, zucchini, turkey or canned tomatoes. If you are new to the world of curries, turn to the "Indian Kitchen Staples" section (page 231) to learn about the more traditional ingredients. While I know not everyone has access to authentic Indian ingredients, these days it is not that tough to spot an Indian grocery store in the neighborhood, or Indian aisle in a supermarket, for all the authentic supplies, thanks to the increase in the cuisine's popularity.

One piece of advice: Adjust the quantity of hot spices, such as red chili powder, green chiles, black pepper or garam masala according to your taste preference. And speaking of adjustments, each recipe in this book makes two generous servings, but if you're feeding more than two people, you can double or even triple the recipes as needed—just keep in mind that the cook times will vary.

I know I am not alone in my passion and obsession for Indian food. So, join me in a journey as we explore the 100 best vibrant, bold, colorful, tantalizing Indian curries through the chapters of this cookbook—all of which are made even better thanks to the Instant Pot. I hope you enjoy re-creating the recipes as much as I've enjoyed creating them.

RESTAURANT-
STYLE
FAVORITES

If you want to explore Indian flavors at home, then start with these forever favorite classics!

After India gained its independence, the native workforce started traveling and settling in different parts of the world. And when we Indians travel, we take our food and culture with us. Result: Today, you will find an Indian restaurant in every nook and corner of your city. These restaurants, mainly the curry houses in Britain, started serving dishes with subtle spices and a creamy gravy sauce; in short, dishes that were more suited for a non-Indian palate. In some way, these dishes were reminders of the bygone colonial era. Over the years, these restaurant-style favorites have become the flag bearer and the identity of Indian cuisine.

Such dishes as Butter Chicken (page 13) and Navratan Korma (page 29) are not part of everyday Indian meals. Even in 2021, as I write this book, a whole generation of people, including my mother, find these dishes not so comforting or wholesome. But you can imagine how popular these Indian restaurant-style favorites are among food lovers worldwide considering the fact that chicken tikka masala was considered the national dish of Britain.

These takeout-style dishes are associated with indulgence, richness and boldness. You will be pleased to know that a plethora of traditional Indian cookware isn't required to make these classic dishes at home. All you need is an Instant Pot and the perfect recipes (which you'll find in this chapter). Thanks to the Instant Pot, it is now so much easier to re-create your Indian restaurant–style favorites at home without spending hours in the kitchen to cook them, followed by tons of utensil cleaning. In fact, the Instant Pot makes such dishes like Dal Makhani (page 21) or Mutton Rogan Josh (page 18) better than any restaurant can.

BUTTER CHICKEN

Boneless Chicken in a Creamy Tomato Gravy

This creamy, orange-ish chicken curry is the harbinger of Indian cuisine worldwide. The dish was developed at a restaurant in New Delhi called Moti Mahal. The chef added leftover roasted chicken pieces to a gravy made with canned tomatoes along with some spices and cream—and voilà, butter chicken was brought into being. Today, the dish is a nationwide phenomenon that refuses to lose its charm even in the twenty-first century. Here is an easy butter chicken recipe that you can make in an Instant Pot without compromising on the flavors.

CHICKEN MARINADE

2 tsp (5 g) Kashmiri red chili powder

1 tbsp (15 ml) fresh lemon juice

1 tsp salt

1 tbsp (1 g) dried fenugreek leaves (kasuri methi)

4 tbsp (60 ml) melted ghee or unsalted butter

2 cups (250 g) boneless, diced chicken (about 9 oz; see note)

GRAVY

4 tbsp (55 g) ghee or unsalted butter, divided

1 cup (160 g) chopped white onion

4 dried Kashmiri chiles

2 tbsp (10 g) chopped fresh ginger

¼ cup (35 g) cashews

1 cup (244 g) canned crushed tomato

¼ cup (65 g) tomato paste or (60 ml) ketchup

1 tsp red chili powder

½ tsp ground cumin

1 tsp salt

½ cup (120 ml) water, divided

¼ cup (60 ml) light cream

¼ tsp garam masala

1 tbsp (1 g) dried fenugreek leaves (kasuri methi)

2 mild green chiles, such as jalapeños, Thai green chiles or serrano peppers, julienned

Prepare the marinade: In a medium-sized bowl, combine the red chili powder, lemon juice, salt, fenugreek leaves and ghee. Mix nicely to form a smooth marinade. Add the chicken pieces and coat with the marinade. Cover and chill in the refrigerator for 2 to 3 hours, or at least 30 minutes.

Prepare the gravy: Set the SAUTÉ mode of the Instant Pot for 6 minutes. Add 2 tablespoons (30 g) of the ghee to the inner pot. Once the ghee is hot, add the onion, Kashmiri chiles, ginger and cashews, and sauté for 2 to 3 minutes, or until the onion turns translucent.

Add the crushed tomato, tomato paste, red chili powder, cumin and salt, and sauté until the timer beeps, or for the next 2 to 3 minutes.

Transfer to a blender. Blend into a smooth paste, using ¼ cup (60 ml) of the water. Pass this curry paste through a sieve to achieve a smooth gravy texture.

Set the SAUTÉ mode for 2 minutes. Add the remaining 2 tablespoons (30 g) of ghee. Once the ghee is hot, add the marinated chicken cubes. Sauté them for 2 minutes.

Next, add the sieved gravy and the remaining ¼ cup (60 ml) of water to the Instant Pot. Stir to mix. Close the lid. Set the steam valve to the sealing position. Pressure cook at high pressure for 5 minutes. Wait for the natural steam release.

Add the cream, garam masala, fenugreek leaves and green chiles. Mix well into the gravy.

Set the SAUTÉ mode to LOW for 2 minutes. Let the curry simmer to thicken a bit.

Serve warm with naan.

NOTE:

❋ Alternatively, you can make butter chicken with leftover rotisserie or roasted chicken. If the chicken is precooked, use the PRESSURE COOK mode for only 2 minutes.

CHANA MASALA
Punjabi-Style Chickpea Curry

Every Indian restaurant has at least one version of *chana masala* on its menu. This typical Punjabi-style chickpea curry is the nation's go-to. It is a filling, wholesome and vegetarian main course dish that tastes divine with fried breads, such as *bhatura* or *poori*, or with naan, as well as with *pulao*. For a delicious restaurant-style chana masala, use dried raw chickpeas instead of precooked canned ones. Follow this tip and you will taste the difference in your chana curry.

SERVES 2
Vegan, Gluten Free

Rinse the chickpeas until the water runs clear. Soak them in about 4 cups (960 ml) of water for 5 to 6 hours, or overnight.

Set the SAUTÉ mode of the Instant Pot for 15 minutes.

Add the oil to the inner pot. Once the oil is hot, add the bay leaf, cardamom pods and cumin seeds. Sauté for a few seconds to release the aroma of the whole spices.

Add the red onion and sauté for 3 to 5 minutes, or until lightly browned.

Add the ginger and garlic paste. Sauté for 30 to 40 seconds for the raw smell to waft away.

Next, add the tomato, salt, turmeric, red chili powder and coriander. Sauté the masala for 2 minutes, or until the masala comes together nicely.

Drain the water from the soaked chickpeas. Add them to the inner pot.

Sauté the chickpeas with the masala until the timer goes off.

Add the water. Stir. Close the lid. Set the steam valve to the sealing position. Pressure cook at high pressure for 40 minutes.

After the natural release of steam, open the lid. Change the Instant Pot setting to SAUTÉ mode for 5 minutes.

Add the green chile, ginger, garam masala, lemon juice and cilantro. Stir to combine. Gently mash the chickpeas, using a ladle, to thicken the sauce and allow the curry to simmer in SAUTÉ mode. Remove and discard the bay leaf before serving.

Serve with your Indian side dish of choice.

1 cup (200 g) dried chickpeas (chana; see note)

4 tbsp (60 ml) vegetable oil

1 bay leaf

2 green cardamom pods

1 black cardamom pod, crushed

1 tsp cumin seeds

1 cup (160 g) chopped red onion

1 tbsp (20 g) ginger and garlic paste

1 cup (180 g) canned tomato

2 tsp (12 g) salt

1 tsp ground turmeric

1 tsp red chili powder or paprika

1 tsp ground coriander

2½ cups (600 ml) water

1 mild green chile, such as jalapeño, Thai green chile or serrano pepper, sliced

1 tbsp (5 g) julienned fresh ginger

1 tsp garam masala

1 tbsp (15 ml) fresh lemon juice

2 tbsp (2 g) chopped fresh cilantro

NOTE:

❋ If you are using canned chickpeas for chana masala, pressure cook them for only 5 minutes to absorb the flavor of the curry.

BUTTER PANEER MASALA

Paneer in a Buttery Gravy

The term *butter masala* describes rich, silky smooth, buttery Indian curries. Butter paneer masala is a classic that you will always spot on the vegetarian section of an Indian restaurant's menu. This magical *makhani* (buttery) masala of mine can be prepared in advance and is freezer-friendly. Now, no need to rush to the nearby Indian restaurant for your favorite butter paneer masala when you can easily make it in an Instant Pot.

1 cup (180 g) canned diced tomato

1 tbsp (16 g) tomato paste

1 tbsp (5 g) chopped fresh ginger

1 tbsp (9 g) cashews

1 mild green chile, such as jalapeño, Thai green chile or serrano pepper, sliced

1¼ tsp (7 g) salt, divided

½ cup (120 ml) water

2 tbsp (28 g) unsalted butter

4 tbsp (60 ml) light cream

1 tsp red chili powder

½ tsp ground turmeric

½ tsp ground cumin

¼ tsp ground green cardamom

1 tsp garam masala

1 tsp dried fenugreek leaves (kasuri methi)

1½ cups (250 g) cubed paneer

1 tbsp (1 g) chopped fresh cilantro

In the inner pot of the Instant Pot, combine the canned tomato, tomato paste, ginger, cashews, green chile, ¼ teaspoon of the salt and the water. Close the lid. Set the steam valve to the sealing position. Pressure cook at high pressure for 2 minutes. Manually release the steam.

Blend the tomato mixture to a smooth paste using an immersion blender, or transfer it to a regular blender and blend into a paste.

Set the SAUTÉ mode of the Instant Pot for 8 minutes. Add the butter to the inner pot. Once the butter is melted, add the blended tomato mixture back to the inner pot along with the cream, remaining teaspoon of salt, red chili powder, turmeric, cumin, cardamom, garam masala and fenugreek leaves, and stir to combine. Let the curry simmer for 5 minutes.

Add the paneer cubes and cilantro. Simmer until the set timer beeps.

Serve with naan.

NOTE:

❋ Alternatively, you can make this butter masala curry with firm tofu or canned chickpeas.

MUTTON ROGAN JOSH

Kashmiri-Style Mutton Curry

One curry that all meat lovers order in an Indian restaurant is *rogan josh*. A bold, robust spicy curry with nothing subtle about it, this recipe has its origin in the Kashmir region of India, where there are two methods of cooking the dish. I am sharing a Kashmiri Pandit-style version cooked without onion, tomato or garlic. Yes, it is possible to cook a flavorful meat curry without using tomato. Instead, the bright color of the curry comes from the dried Kashmiri red chiles.

SERVES 2

Gluten Free

❖

Using a mortar and pestle or spice grinder, make a coarse powder of the cardamom pods and cloves, then set aside.

Wash, clean and pat the lamb pieces dry. Set aside.

Set the SAUTÉ mode of the Instant Pot for 15 minutes.

Add the oil to the inner pot. Once the oil is hot, add the cumin seeds and asafetida.

Add the lamb pieces. Sauté for 6 to 8 minutes, or until the fat of the lamb is released and the meat is lightly browned.

Next, add the red chili powder, turmeric, fennel, ground ginger, coriander and salt, and fry for 1 minute.

Whisk the dahi until it is smooth and lump free. Add it slowly, stirring, to the inner pot to prevent lump formation; don't dump it all in at once. Sauté for 3 minutes.

Add the water and stir to combine. Close the lid. Set the steam valve to the sealing position. Pressure cook at high pressure for 20 minutes. After the timer beeps, wait for the natural release of steam.

In a small bowl, soak the saffron in the tablespoon (15 ml) of warm water.

Check the lamb pieces for doneness. Add the soaked saffron with its liquid, fresh ginger, the prepared spice powder and cilantro. Set the SAUTÉ mode for 5 minutes and simmer the curry.

Serve with basmati pilaf.

NOTE:

❖ Lamb rib, hind leg or any low-fat pieces work best for this curry. You can make it with boneless meat as well.

1 black cardamom pod

4 green cardamom pods

4 whole cloves

9 oz (250 g) bone-in lamb, cut into 1½" to 2" (4- to 5-cm) pieces (see note)

¼ cup (60 ml) mustard oil

1 tsp cumin seeds

½ tsp asafetida

2 tsp (5 g) Kashmiri red chili powder

½ tsp ground turmeric

1 tsp ground fennel

1 tsp ground ginger

1 tsp ground coriander

1 tsp salt

1 cup (240 ml) dahi (curd) or plain Greek yogurt

2 cups (480 ml) water

1 tsp saffron strands

1 tbsp (15 ml) warm water

1 tbsp (5 g) julienned fresh ginger

2 tbsp (2 g) chopped fresh cilantro

DAL MAKHANI

Creamy Three-Legume Curry

The renowned chef of the Moti Mahal restaurant in Delhi wanted to create a vegetarian counterpart to butter chicken. Hence, he developed a creamy, rich, indulgent *dal makhani* recipe. Traditionally, the legumes were slow cooked overnight to get a velvety, buttery mouthfeel. I fell in love with dal makhani all over again after making it with the SLOW COOK mode of an Instant Pot. Try it once and you will forget the dal makhani from your favorite Indian restaurant.

1 cup (200 g) dried whole black gram lentils (sabut urad dal)

¼ cup (50 g) dried red kidney beans (rajma)

¼ cup (50 g) dried split chickpeas (chana dal)

6 cups (1.4 L) water, divided

4 tbsp (55 g) ghee

1 bay leaf

4 whole cloves

1 black cardamom pod, crushed

¼ tsp asafetida

1 cup (160 g) finely chopped yellow onion

1 tbsp (20 g) ginger and garlic paste

1 cup (244 g) canned crushed tomato

1 tbsp (16 g) tomato paste

2 tsp (12 g) salt

2 tsp (5 g) red chili powder

1 tsp ground coriander

¼ tsp ground turmeric

4 tbsp (60 ml) light cream

1 tsp garam masala

2 mild green chiles, such as jalapeños, Thai green chiles or serrano peppers, thinly sliced

1 tbsp (1 g) dried fenugreek leaves (kasuri methi)

1 tbsp (1 g) chopped fresh cilantro

¼ cup (60 ml) water or milk, to thin if needed

1 tbsp (14 g) unsalted butter

Rinse the lentils, beans and chickpeas until the water runs clear. Soak them together in the same bowl in about 4 cups (960 ml) of water for 5 to 6 hours, or overnight.

Set the SAUTÉ mode of the Instant Pot for 12 minutes. Add the ghee to the inner pot. Once the ghee is hot, add the bay leaf, cloves, cardamom pod, asafetida and onion. Sauté until the onion becomes golden.

Add the ginger and garlic paste. Sauté for 30 to 40 seconds.

Add the crushed tomato, tomato paste, salt, red chili powder, coriander and turmeric. Sauté for 2 minutes.

Drain the water from the soaked legumes. Add them to the inner pot.

Sauté the legumes for 3 to 5 minutes, or until the timer beeps. Add the remaining 2 cups (480 ml) of water. Stir to combine.

Set the Instant Pot to SLOW COOK mode and cook the dal makhani for 8 hours, or overnight.

Once the legumes are soft and fully cooked, add the cream, garam masala, green chiles, fenugreek leaves and cilantro, and stir to combine. If the dal makhani seems too thick, use up to ¼ cup (60 ml) of water or milk to get the desired consistency.

Set the SAUTÉ mode for 5 minutes. Simmer the dal makhani and gently mash the legumes, using the back of the ladle.

Add the butter. Remove and discard the bay leaf before serving. Serve with *lachha paratha* or naan.

Mughlai-Style Egg Curry

Boiled Eggs in a Creamy Golden Gravy

SERVES 2

Gluten Free

Like chicken curries, the list of Indian egg curries is endless. My personal favorite is this Mughlai-style egg curry. Restaurant-style flavor, luscious texture and the easiest cooking method are the highlights of this recipe. I hope, like me, you are also using your Instant Pot to boil eggs. If not, then start right away!

Soak the saffron in the tablespoon (15 ml) of warm water. Set aside.

Set the SAUTÉ mode of the Instant Pot for 5 minutes.

Add the ghee to the inner pot. Once the ghee is hot, add the caraway seeds and onion, and fry until the onion becomes translucent, 2 to 3 minutes. Add the ginger, green chile and almonds, and sauté for 1 minute. Add ¼ cup (60 ml) of the water and mix. Close the lid. Set the steam valve to the sealing position. Pressure cook at high pressure for 2 minutes. Manually release the steam.

Transfer to a blender and blend the mixture to a smooth paste.

Set the SAUTÉ mode again for 8 minutes. Transfer the curry paste back to the inner pot and stir.

Next, add the red chili powder, salt, turmeric, cream, soaked saffron with its liquid and the remaining ¾ cup (180 ml) of water. Let the curry simmer for 1 minute.

Add the halved boiled eggs and gently stir to mix them into the curry sauce. Simmer until the timer beeps.

Garnish with the cilantro and almond slivers.

¼ tsp saffron threads

1 tbsp (15 ml) warm water

4 tbsp (55 g) ghee

1 tsp caraway seeds

½ cup (80 g) sliced yellow onion

1 tbsp (5 g) chopped fresh ginger

1 mild green chile, such as jalapeño, Thai green chile or serrano pepper, chopped

2 tbsp (18 g) almonds, skinned

1 cup (240 ml) water, divided

1 tsp red chili powder

1 tsp salt

½ tsp ground turmeric

2 tbsp (30 ml) light cream

4 hard-boiled large eggs, peeled and halved

1 tbsp (1 g) chopped fresh cilantro, for garnish

1 tsp almond slivers, for garnish

DUM ALOO

Mughlai-Style Fried Potato Curry

Potatoes came to India with the Portuguese during the seventeenth century, but ever since then, they have effortlessly become a part of our cuisine. When it comes to restaurant-style favorites, every potato lover's delight, *dum aloo*, cannot be missed. This rich, slow cooked potato curry in a thick Mughlai-style masala also has Kashmiri, Bengali and Punjabi versions. My dum aloo recipe is a restaurant-style variant of the dish that you can easily make in an Instant Pot without spending hours in the kitchen.

9 oz (250 g) baby potatoes, peeled (see note)

2 tsp (12 g) salt, divided

1½ tsp (3 g) ground turmeric, divided

1½ tsp (3 g) red chili powder, divided

¼ cup (35 g) cashews

½ cup (120 ml) hot water

4 tbsp (60 ml) vegetable oil, divided

1 bay leaf

2 dried red chiles, such as Kashmiri

1 tsp cumin seeds

1 cup (160 g) finely chopped yellow onion

1 tbsp (20 g) ginger and garlic paste

1 cup (240 ml) dahi (curd) or plain Greek yogurt

1½ cups (360 ml) water

1 tsp garam masala

1 tbsp (1 g) dried fenugreek leaves (kasuri methi)

1 tbsp (1 g) chopped fresh cilantro

NOTE:

❁ You can make dum aloo with regular-sized potatoes as well. Just cut each potato into quarters or chunks.

In a medium-sized bowl, coat the potatoes with ½ teaspoon of the salt, ½ teaspoon of the turmeric and ½ teaspoon of the red chili powder. Mix nicely. Set aside.

Soak the cashews in the hot water for 10 minutes. Transfer them to a blender with their water and blend into a smooth paste.

Set the SAUTÉ mode of the Instant Pot for 6 minutes.

Add 2 tablespoons (30 ml) of the oil to the inner pot. Once the oil is hot, add the spice-coated baby potatoes.

Fry for 6 minutes, or until they turn a bit crisp and golden on the outside. Transfer to a plate and set aside.

Set the SAUTÉ mode for 10 minutes. Add the remaining 2 tablespoons (30 ml) of oil, bay leaf, dried red chiles, cumin seeds and onion. Sauté for 3 to 4 minutes, or until the onion is lightly golden.

Add the ginger and garlic paste. Sauté for 30 to 40 seconds.

Whisk the dahi with the remaining teaspoon of turmeric and teaspoon of red chili powder to a smooth, lump-free paste.

Add the whisked masala dahi to the inner pot along with the remaining 1½ teaspoons (9 g) of salt. Stir to combine. Sauté for 2 to 3 minutes while stirring constantly to prevent lump formation.

Add the fried baby potatoes, cashew paste and 1½ cups (360 ml) of water, and stir to combine. Close the lid. Set the steam valve to the sealing position. Pressure cook the curry for 10 minutes at the normal setting. Wait for the natural release of steam. Check the potatoes for doneness.

Add the garam masala, fenugreek leaves and cilantro. Stir to combine. Remove and discard the bay leaf before serving.

Serve with your Indian flatbread of choice.

Vegan Tikka Masala

Tikka Masala with a Meat Substitute

Chicken tikka masala is one of the modern recipes developed in Britain as a result of fusion culture. Today, we have all sorts of tikka masala gravy versions—paneer, mushroom, chickpea or tofu—but one of my recent favorites is vegan tikka masala. The texture and taste of vegan, mock meat made from soybeans is very close to boneless chicken. Hence, the dish is a true delight for the vegan food lovers who miss tikka masala from their favorite Indian restaurant.

SERVES 2

Vegan, Gluten Free

Prepare the marinade: In a medium-sized bowl, combine the cashew cream, mustard oil, ginger and garlic paste, red chili powder, turmeric, cumin, salt and lemon juice. Whisk to form a smooth, lump-free mixture.

Place the mock meat in the bowl and coat nicely in the marinade. Cover and chill in the refrigerator overnight, or for at least 1 hour.

To cook the mock meat, add the ½ cup (120 ml) of vegetable oil to the inner pot of the Instant Pot and set the sauté mode for 10 minutes. Once the oil is hot, arrange the marinated mock meat in a single layer in the pot and let it cook. Once the meat is slightly crisp on one side, turn it over and cook the other side. When the time is up, transfer the mock meat to a plate and set aside.

Prepare the gravy: Set the sauté mode of the Instant Pot for 8 minutes. Add 2 tablespoons (30 ml) of the vegetable oil to the inner pot. Once the oil is hot, arrange the cooked mock meat in the pot. Do not overcrowd the pot. Once crisp on one side, flip to the other side. Transfer to a plate. Cover with aluminum foil. Set aside.

Set the sauté mode for 10 minutes. Add the remaining 2 tablespoons (30 ml) of vegetable oil to the inner pot. Add the red chiles, onion and ginger. Sauté for 3 minutes, or until the onion is lightly browned.

Add the canned tomato, cashews, tomato paste, salt, turmeric, red chili powder and cumin. Sauté for 2 for 3 minutes for the masala to come together.

(continued)

1 cup (200 g) mock meat, cut into bite-sized cubes (see note)

½ cup (120 ml) vegetable oil

MARINADE

¼ cup (60 ml) cashew cream

2 tbsp (30 ml) mustard oil

1 tbsp (20 g) ginger and garlic paste

1 tsp Kashmiri red chili powder

½ tsp ground turmeric

1 tsp ground cumin

1 tsp salt

1 tbsp (15 ml) fresh lemon juice

GRAVY

4 tbsp (60 ml) vegetable oil, divided

2 dried Kashmiri red chiles

1 cup (160 g) finely chopped yellow onion

1 tbsp (5 g) chopped fresh ginger

1 cup (244 g) canned crushed tomato

¼ cup (35 g) cashews

1 tbsp (16 g) tomato paste

1 tsp salt

½ tsp ground turmeric

½ tsp red chili powder or paprika

½ tsp ground cumin

Add the water. Stir to mix. Close the lid. Set the steam valve to the sealing position. Pressure cook at high pressure for 2 minutes. Manually release the steam. Blend the mixture to a paste using an immersion blender or a regular blender.

To the inner pot, add the curry paste, cashew cream, garam masala, fenugreek leaves and green chile, and stir to combine. Add the grilled mock meat.

Close the lid. Set the steam valve to the sealing position. Pressure cook at high pressure for 2 minutes. Wait for the natural release of the steam.

Garnish with the cilantro. Serve with naan.

NOTE:

✳ **You can also make this vegan tikka masala with soybean tempeh, soy curls or jackfruit.**

¼ cup (60 ml) water

1 tbsp (15 ml) cashew cream

1 tsp garam masala

1 tbsp (1 g) dried fenugreek leaves (kasuri methi)

1 mild green chile, such as jalapeño, Thai green chile or serrano pepper, sliced

1 tbsp (1 g) chopped fresh cilantro, for garnish

NAVRATAN KORMA

Vegetable Curry with Nine Gems

Mughali cuisine is known for its over-the-top ingredients, cooking style and fineness. *Navratan* is a Sanskrit term for "nine gems." This vegetarian curry has nine special ingredients that make it befitting of a royal feast. It is the combination of vegetables, fruits, paneer, whole spices, nuts and saffron. The cooking technique to make a fabulous navratan korma is to build on the layers of flavor. Sadly, many restaurants nowadays dump it all together and make it like any other takeaway curry. I am sharing with you a recipe that will guide you on how to build layers of flavors in a navratan korma that is cooked in an Instant Pot.

¼ cup (35 g) cashews

1 tbsp (9 g) white poppy seeds

1 tbsp (12 g) melon seeds

¼ cup (60 ml) hot water

4 tbsp (55 g) ghee

1 cup (160 g) sliced yellow onion

1 tbsp (5 g) chopped fresh ginger

2 green cardamom pods

1 (1" [2.5-cm]-long piece cinnamon stick

1 bay leaf

1 tsp salt

1 tsp red chili powder

¼ cup (33 g) diced carrot

¼ cup (25 g) sliced green beans, cut into ½" (1.3-cm) pieces

¼ cup (42 g) diced potato

¼ cup (37 g) green peas, fresh or frozen

½ cup (50 g) cauliflower florets

¼ cup (40 g) diced pineapple (see note)

¼ cup (60 ml) water

Soak the cashews and poppy and melon seeds in the ¼ cup (60 ml) of hot water. Cover and set aside.

Set the SAUTÉ mode of the Instant Pot for 15 minutes.

Add the ghee to the inner pot. Once the ghee is hot, add the onion, ginger, cardamom pods, cinnamon stick and bay leaf. Fry until the onion becomes golden.

Discard the bay leaf and cinnamon stick. In a blender, blend the onion, cardamom and cashew and seed mixture (with its liquid) to a smooth paste.

Add the blended paste back to the inner pot along with the salt, red chili powder, carrot, green beans, potato, green peas, cauliflower, pineapple and ¼ cup (60 ml) of water. Stir to combine.

NOTE:

❋ You can replace the pineapple with dried apricots or skip adding it.

(continued)

1 cup (240 ml) milk

½ tsp garam masala

1 tsp dried fenugreek leaves (kasuri methi)

1 mild green chile, such as jalapeño, Thai green chile or serrano pepper, sliced

¼ tsp saffron strands

1 tbsp (7 g) almond slivers, for garnish

1 tbsp (1 g) chopped fresh cilantro, for garnish

Close the lid. Set the steam valve to the sealing position. Pressure cook at high pressure for 5 minutes. Wait for the natural release of steam.

Add the milk, garam masala, fenugreek leaves, green chile and saffron. Set the SAUTÉ mode for 5 minutes to simmer the curry.

Garnish with the almond slivers and cilantro. Serve with naan.

DAL TADKA

Restaurant-Style Dal Curry

Tadka is the Hindi term for "tempering"—a glaze of hot ghee plus whole or ground spices. *Dal tadka* is the forever favorite yellow dal with a rich tempering of ghee, cumin seeds, garlic and red chiles on top. When it comes to tadka, there are no set rules. From cumin seeds, mustard seeds, onion and garlic to dried red chiles or curry leaves, you can take your pick. But one ingredient that is the soul of a good dal tadka is ghee (clarified butter). The rich sweetness of the ghee fat combined with the protein create a feeling of true ambrosia.

SERVES 2

Vegetarian, Gluten Free

❋

Rinse the pigeon peas and moong beans until the water runs clear. Soak in water for 15 minutes.

Meanwhile, set the SAUTÉ mode of the Instant Pot for 10 minutes.

Add the ghee to the inner pot. Once the ghee is hot, add the red onion and ginger, and sauté for 3 minutes, or until the onion is lightly browned.

Add the tomato, green chile, salt, turmeric and red chili powder, and sauté for 2 to 3 minutes.

Drain all the water from the soaked legumes. Add them to the inner pot.

Add the fresh water. Stir. Close the lid. Set the steam valve to the sealing position. Pressure cook at high pressure for 10 minutes. Wait for the natural release of the steam, or if you're in a hurry, you can manually release the pressure.

Gently mash the dal, using the ladle, to thicken it a bit.

Prepare the tempering: Heat the 2 tablespoons (28 g) of ghee in a skillet over low to medium heat, and add the asafetida, cumin, red chiles and garlic.

Fry for 2 for 3 minutes, or until the garlic is lightly golden. Make sure it is not burning.

Pour this tempering over the dal (see note). Add the cilantro and lemon juice, and stir to combine. Seal the Instant Pot with a lid and let the dal sit for 5 minutes for the aroma and flavor of the ghee and tadka to combine.

Serve with jeera rice.

1 cup (170 g) dried split pigeon peas (toor dal)

¼ cup (50 g) dried split yellow moong beans (moong dal)

2 tbsp (28 g) ghee

1 cup (160 g) chopped red onion

1 tbsp (5 g) chopped fresh ginger

½ cup (90 g) chopped tomato

1 green chile, such as jalapeño, Thai green chile or serrano pepper, chopped

2 tsp (12 g) salt

1 tsp ground turmeric

1 tsp red chili powder

2 cups (480 ml) water

1 tbsp (1 g) finely chopped fresh cilantro

1 tbsp (15 ml) fresh lemon juice

TEMPERING (TADKA)

2 tbsp (28 g) ghee

¼ tsp asafetida

1 tsp cumin seeds

2 dried red chiles, such as Kashmiri

1 tbsp (10 g) chopped garlic

NOTE:

❋ If you are not too keen on adding tadka separately, you can add the tempering ingredients before the red onion and cook them with the legumes.

SHAHI PANEER

Creamy and Rich Paneer Curry

The dish is the symbol of Mughlai cuisine in Indian restaurants. The soft cubes of paneer cooked in a typical Mughal-style creamy, sweet, rich gravy with a subtle scent perfectly defines *shahi paneer*. The term *shahi* indicates the fineness of the dish, befitting of a royal feast. The beautiful color of the gravy comes from the addition of Kashmiri red chiles and saffron. Soaking saffron in warm water releases its color and aroma.

¼ tsp saffron strands, plus more for garnish

1 tbsp (15 ml) warm water

2 tbsp (28 g) ghee or unsalted butter

1 tsp cumin seeds

½ tsp fennel seeds

1 bay leaf

1 (1" [2.5-cm])-long piece cinnamon stick

1 black cardamom pod

4 green cardamom pods

2 dried Kashmiri red chiles

½ cup (80 g) finely chopped yellow onion

1 tbsp (5 g) chopped fresh ginger

1 tbsp (10 g) chopped garlic

1 tbsp (9 g) cashews

1 tbsp (9 g) blanched and skinless almonds

1 cup (180 g) chopped tomato

2 dried apricots, chopped

1 tsp ground turmeric

1½ tsp (9 g) salt

½ tsp red chili powder

1¼ cups (300 ml) water, divided

¼ cup (60 ml) light cream, plus 1 tbsp (15 ml) for garnish

1 tsp dried fenugreek leaves (kasuri methi)

9 oz (250 g) paneer, cut into triangles

1 tbsp (1 g) chopped fresh cilantro, for garnish

Soak the saffron in the warm water. Set aside.

Set the SAUTÉ mode of the Instant Pot for 10 minutes.

Add the ghee to the inner pot. Once the ghee is hot, add the cumin, fennel seeds, bay leaf, cinnamon stick, cardamom pods and red chiles. Sauté for 20 seconds.

Add the onion, ginger and garlic and sauté for 3 minutes, or until the onion is lightly browned.

Add the cashews and almonds, tomato, dried apricots, turmeric, salt and red chili powder. Sauté until the timer beeps. Add ¼ cup (60 ml) of the water. Stir to combine.

Close the lid. Set the steam valve to the sealing position. Pressure cook at high pressure for 2 minutes. Manually release the steam. Discard the bay leaf.

Transfer to a blender and blend the mixture until completely smooth and creamy (see note).

Add the curry paste back to the inner pot. Add the remaining cup (240 ml) of water, cream, soaked saffron and its liquid and fenugreek leaves. Stir to combine.

Set the SAUTÉ mode for 5 minutes. Add the paneer pieces. Let the curry simmer until the timer beeps.

Garnish with the fresh cilantro, saffron strands and cream. Serve with naan for an indulgent curry night.

NOTE:

✤ For a silky smooth texture of the gravy, you can pass it through a sieve after blending.

Chicken Balti

Britain's Curry House–Style Chicken Curry

The name of this chicken curry has many stories around it. Some believe it to have its origin in a region of Pakistan called Baltistan; some credit a restaurant in Birmingham, England, called Adil; whereas others say the word *balti* is for the special pan used for making and serving the chicken curry. But in plain words, chicken balti is a flavorsome Indian chicken curry that is so easy to make in an Instant Pot. You will find one or the other type of balti dishes in almost all the Indian restaurants in Britain. Surprisingly, in India, I have not once tasted or spotted balti chicken in any of the restaurants.

Set the SAUTÉ mode of the Instant Pot for 15 minutes.

Add the oil to the inner pot. Once the oil is hot, add the bay leaf and onion. Fry the onion for 3 to 4 minutes, or until lightly golden. Add the ginger and garlic. Sauté for 40 to 50 seconds, or until the raw smell wafts away.

Add the crushed tomato, tomato paste, curry powder, cumin, salt and green chiles, and sauté for the next 2 to 3 minutes, or until the tomato breaks down.

Add the chicken pieces. Sauté for 5 minutes, or until they become almost opaque.

Add the water. Stir to mix. Close the lid. Set the steam valve to the sealing position. Pressure cook at high pressure for 2 minutes. Wait for the natural release of steam. Add the whisked dahi and garam masala, and simmer in SAUTÉ mode for 5 minutes. Remove and discard the bay leaf before serving.

Garnish with the cilantro and serve.

4 tbsp (60 ml) vegetable oil

1 bay leaf

1 cup (160 g) finely chopped yellow onion

1 tbsp (5 g) finely chopped fresh ginger

1 tbsp (10 g) finely chopped garlic

1 cup (244 g) canned crushed tomato

2 tbsp (32 g) tomato paste or puree

1 tbsp (6 g) curry powder

1 tsp ground cumin

1¼ tsp (7 g) salt

2 green chiles, such as jalapeños, Thai green chiles or serrano peppers, chopped

9 oz (250 g) boneless chicken, cut into bite-sized pieces

½ cup (120 ml) water

¼ cup (60 ml) dahi (curd) or plain Greek yogurt, whisked

1 tsp garam masala

1 tbsp (1 g) chopped fresh cilantro, for garnish

PANEER IN WHITE GRAVY

Paneer in a White Sauce

In many Indian restaurants, the gravies are color-categorized as orange, white or brown. The delicious onion and cashew gravy (a white one) with mild spiciness is always my favorite. This gravy tastes delicious with lachha paratha or any other crispy Indian bread. At home, you can add your protein of choice to this gravy if you are not a huge fan of paneer.

1 cup (160 g) chopped white onion

¼ cup (35 g) cashews

4 green cardamom pods

1 mild green chile, such as jalapeño, Thai green chile or serrano pepper, chopped

1¼ tsp (7 g) salt, divided

1 cup (240 ml) water, plus up to ¼ cup (60 ml) if needed

½ cup (120 ml) milk

1 tsp garam masala

1 tsp freshly ground black pepper

1 tsp dried fenugreek leaves (kasuri methi)

2 tbsp (10 g) julienned fresh ginger

1½ cups (250 g) cubed paneer

1 tbsp (1 g) chopped fresh cilantro, for garnish

In the inner pot of the Instant Pot, combine the onion, cashews, cardamom pods, green chile, ¼ teaspoon of the salt and the cup (240 ml) of water.

Close the lid. Set the steam valve to the sealing position. Pressure cook at high pressure for 2 minutes. Manually release the steam.

Blend the pressure-cooked ingredients to a smooth paste using an immersion blender or in a regular blender.

Add the curry paste back to the Instant Pot along with the milk, garam masala, black pepper, fenugreek leaves, ginger and remaining teaspoon of salt, or to taste. Stir to combine.

Set the SAUTÉ mode for 6 minutes. Once the curry starts to simmer, add the paneer cubes, stir to mix and simmer until the timer beeps. If the curry seems too thick, add up to ¼ cup (60 ml) of water to get your desired consistency.

Garnish with the fresh cilantro. Serve with naan.

MUTTON KORMA
Old Delhi–Style Meat Curry

Korma originated in Central India during the Mughal reign. In the royal kitchen of Mughals, a variety of kormas were prepared and served. The meat-searing technique, the combination of aromatics and the right cut of meat differentiate an excellent korma from an average thick gravy. This korma recipe is inspired by the Awadhi-style korma masala from Lucknow, the city of nawabs, curated with perfection for cooking in an Instant Pot.

SERVES 2

Gluten Free

Clean and pat the meat pieces dry.

Prepare the marinade: In a medium-sized bowl, combine the dahi, ginger and garlic paste, red chili powder, coriander, garam masala and salt. Add the meat and coat each piece with the marinade. Cover and chill in the refrigerator overnight or for at least 1 hour.

Prepare the gravy: Soak the saffron in the warm milk. Set aside.

Set the SAUTÉ mode of the Instant Pot for 15 minutes.

Add the ghee to the inner pot. Once the ghee is hot, add the onion and fry until it becomes golden.

Next, add the poppy seeds, cashews, cardamom pods, cinnamon stick and cloves. Sauté for 1 minute. Transfer the mixture to a blender. Blend into a smooth paste, using 1 to 2 tablespoons (15 to 30 ml) of the water.

Meanwhile, add the marinated meat to the inner pot. Sear until the fat of the meat is released and the pieces are well browned, about 5 minutes.

Add the onion paste, remaining water, red chili powder and salt.

Close the lid. Set the steam valve to the sealing position. Pressure cook at high pressure for 20 minutes. Wait for the natural release of the steam.

Add the soaked saffron with its soaking liquid, kewra and green chiles. Set the SAUTÉ mode for 5 minutes for the aromatics to flavor the curry.

Garnish with the cilantro. Serve with naan or pilaf.

NOTE:

❋ Kewra water is an edible flavor essence used in Indian cuisine. It adds a subtle sweet aroma to the curry. You can skip adding kewra essence to the korma. Instead you can add ground green cardamom.

9 oz (250 g) bone-in goat meat, cut into 2" (5-cm) pieces

MARINADE

½ cup (120 ml) dahi (curd) or plain Greek yogurt, whisked

1 tbsp (20 g) ginger and garlic paste

½ tsp Kashmiri red chili powder

1 tsp ground coriander

1 tsp garam masala

1 tsp salt

GRAVY

¼ tsp saffron strands

1 tbsp (15 ml) warm milk

⅓ cup (76 g) ghee

1 cup (160 g) sliced yellow onion

1 tsp white poppy seeds

1 tbsp (9 g) cashews

4 green cardamom pods

1 black cardamom pod

1 (1" [2.5-cm])-long piece cinnamon stick

4 whole cloves

1 cup (240 ml) water, divided

1 tsp Kashmiri red chili powder

2 tsp (12 g) salt

¼ tsp kewra essence (see note)

2 mild green chiles, such as jalapeños, Thai green chiles or serrano peppers, sliced

2 tbsp (2 g) chopped fresh cilantro, for garnish

A BAG OF BEANS

India is not only one of the largest producers of pulses, but also the biggest consumer. And it is clearly visible in Indian recipes. There are so many vegetarian curries packed with legumes. Whereas vegan enthusiasts are now awakening to the power of plant-based protein, in India, lentils and other legumes have been consumed in various creative ways for centuries.

In the Hindi language, any curry with lentils is called *dal* or *dhal*. We have dal recipes for every mood, every season and every occasion. From the first solid food of a newborn to a good-bye funeral feast, dal is omnipresent in the life of every Indian. We take great pride in talking about our Langar Wali Dal (page 53) or Punjabi Rajma Masala (page 46). But those are just the tip of the iceberg. In an Indian kitchen, there are typically more than 15 varieties of legumes used for making everyday meals.

Legumes and stovetop pressure cookers are an age-old affair in an Indian kitchen. When I brought home my first Instant Pot, the Indian in me was reluctant to take the leap of faith and accept the change. I was afraid that an Instant Pot would not give me the desired taste and texture, and that the process would be too complicated to make a simple dal. I also thought it would be upsetting to my late great-grandmother, who never approved of pressure-cooked dals because of their texture. It wasn't easy to part ways with my beloved stovetop pressure cooker, which was a wedding gift. There were so many food memories, nostalgia and emotions etched into that gadget. But I finally took the leap of faith!

I am happy to admit that my journey from the traditional pressure cooker to the Instant Pot for making dals was an enlightening one. Once you get the basic dal right, the creative possibilities are endless. I started with simple recipes, such as Zucchini Moong Dal (page 45) and Sabut Masoor Dal (page 54), and eventually graduated to making the family heirloom recipes, such as the Langar Wali Dal. All the recipes in this chapter are custom made for Instant Pot cooking. Each is unique in taste and texture, and will give you a whole new perspective about how to cook lentils and other legumes to perfection in an Instant Pot.

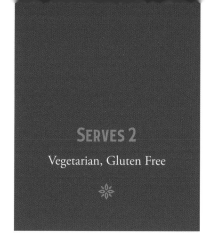

ZUCCHINI MOONG DAL

Yellow Moong Beans with Zucchini

Any type of squash and legume are a match made in heaven. A few commonly added squashes in an Indian curry are bottle gourd, ridge gourd, bitter gourd and winter squash. I had never tasted any other kind of squash until a decade back, when I came across other popular squash varieties, such as zucchini. To my surprise, the subtle, sweet flavor of zucchini blends perfectly with a delicate yellow moong dal. It is healthy and easy to digest. Zucchini moong dal cooks in an Instant Pot in under 15 minutes and is perfect with rice for a weeknight family dinner.

1 cup (200 g) dried split yellow moong beans (moong dal)

2 tbsp (28 g) ghee

1 tbsp (10 g) minced garlic

1 whole dried red chile, such as Kashmiri

⅓ cup (53 g) finely chopped red onion

1 tsp ground turmeric

1 tsp red chili powder

1½ tsp (9 g) salt, or to taste

1 cup (124 g) diced zucchini

2 cups (480 ml) water, at room temperature

½ tsp garam masala

2 tbsp (2 g) chopped fresh cilantro

Rinse the moong beans until the water runs clear, then soak them in water for 10 minutes.

Set the SAUTÉ mode of the Instant Pot for 10 minutes.

Add the ghee to the inner pot. Once the ghee is hot, add the garlic and dried red chile. Sauté until the aroma of the garlic is released and it is lightly browned, 20 to 30 seconds.

Next, add the red onion and fry for 1 to 2 minutes, or until lightly browned, stirring to prevent the onion and garlic from burning.

Drain all the water from the soaked beans. Add them to the inner pot and fry for 1 minute, stirring at regular intervals.

Add the turmeric, red chili powder, salt and zucchini. Stir to mix, then add the water.

One last time, give the dal a good stir and taste. If needed, add more salt or seasoning.

Close the lid. Set the steam valve to the sealing position. Set the PRESSURE COOK mode for 5 minutes at the normal setting. After the timer beeps, let the steam release naturally.

Open the lid, add the garam masala and cilantro, and stir to combine.

Serve with rice for a wholesome Indian meal.

NOTE:

❉ You can make this dal with any type of squash, such as yellow summer squash, butternut or honeynut squash, field pumpkin and so on.

Punjabi Rajma Masala

Red Kidney Beans Curry

A robust, vibrant, nutritious curry of red kidney beans (*rajma*) from the land of five rivers, Punjab, is a forever favorite lunch staple in India. The combination of rajma with rice, known as *rajma chawal*, is my soul food. Rajma masala is a vegan, gluten-free curry that will remind you of a Mexican-style red kidney bean chili. And Instant Pot *rajma masala* is my husband's favorite because of its perfect texture and taste. In an Instant Pot, the flavor of the curry penetrates within the red kidney beans, making them juicy and so delicious.

SERVES 2

Vegan, Gluten Free

Rinse the red kidney beans with water. Next, soak them in enough water to cover for 5 to 6 hours or overnight.

Set the SAUTÉ mode of the Instant Pot for 15 minutes. Add the oil to the inner pot. Once the oil is hot, add the red onion and fry until lightly browned, 3 to 5 minutes.

Add the ginger and garlic paste, then stir and fry the masala for 1 minute, or until the raw smell wafts away.

Drain the water from the soaked beans. Add them to the Instant Pot along with the salt, red chili powder, coriander and turmeric. Stir to combine, and fry the beans until the sauté time is over, about 5 minutes.

Add the water and tomato, and give the beans a good stir.

Close the lid. Set the steam valve to the sealing position. Pressure cook at high pressure for 25 minutes. Once the timer beeps, let the steam release naturally.

Open the lid. Check the beans for doneness—they should be soft and fully cooked. Add the garam masala, fenugreek leaves, green chiles and cilantro. Stir to combine.

Set the SAUTÉ mode for 5 minutes to simmer and thicken the rajma masala gravy before serving.

Serve with steamed basmati rice for a truly Punjabi-style meal.

1½ cups (300 g) dried red kidney beans (rajma; see note)

4 tbsp (60 ml) vegetable oil

1 cup (160 g) finely chopped red onion

1 tbsp (20 g) ginger and garlic paste

2 tsp (12 g) salt

1 tsp red chili powder or paprika

1 tsp ground coriander

1 tsp ground turmeric

2 cups (480 ml) water

1 cup (180 g) chopped tomato (see note)

1 tsp garam masala

1 tsp dried fenugreek leaves (kasuri methi)

2 mild green chiles, such as jalapeños, Thai green chiles or serrano peppers, sliced

2 tbsp (2 g) chopped fresh cilantro

NOTE:

❋ Alternatively, you can make rajma masala with 1½ cups (384 g) of drained and rinsed canned beans. Follow the rest of the recipe instructions as written, but pressure cook the canned beans for only 3 minutes.

SHAHI DAL
Mughlai-Style Black Lentil Curry

Shahi dal, as the name suggests, is an aromatic, and delicious Mughlai-style dish of split black gram lentils (*chilka urad dal*) cooked with milk, ghee and a fistful of dried fruits. This lentil curry has subtle notes of sweetness along with the richness of such ingredients as ghee and almonds. Serve it with naan, lachha paratha or jeera rice for an indulgent Indian dinner.

1 cup (180 g) dried split black lentils (chilka urad dal)

2 green cardamom pods

1 whole bay leaf

¼ cup (45 g) chopped tomato

1 tsp ginger and garlic paste

2 mild green chiles, such as jalapeños, Thai green chiles or serrano peppers, finely chopped

1 tsp salt

1 tsp red chili powder

1 tsp ground turmeric

1¼ cups (300 ml) water

¼ cup (60 ml) milk

1 tsp garam masala

1 tbsp (1 g) chopped fresh cilantro, for garnish

TEMPERING (TADKA)

1 tbsp (14 g) ghee

1 tsp cumin seeds

1 tbsp (7 g) sliced almonds

1 tbsp (9 g) chopped golden raisins

Rinse the lentils until the water runs clear. Soak them in water for 5 to 6 hours or overnight.

After the soak time is up, you will notice the black husk of lentils starting to leave the white skin underneath. Rub the dal between your palms to remove the black husks. Rinse again and you will end up with a mainly white-skinned dal with a few black peels here and there. Drain all the water from the soaked lentils.

In the inner pot of the Instant Pot, combine the drained lentils, cardamom pods, bay leaf, tomato, ginger and garlic paste, green chiles, salt, red chili powder, turmeric and water. Close the lid and set the steam valve to the sealing position.

Pressure cook at high pressure for 20 minutes. Wait for the natural release of steam. Open the lid, add the milk and garam masala, and gently stir, using the back of a ladle, to mix the dal. Let it simmer in SAUTÉ mode for 5 minutes. Remove and discard the bay leaf.

Meanwhile, prepare the tempering: In a small skillet, heat the ghee over medium heat. Add the cumin seeds, sliced almonds and raisins, and fry until lightly golden, about 5 minutes. Pour this tempering over the dal.

Garnish with the cilantro and serve.

Garlicky Butternut Squash Dal

Yellow Moong Bean Curry with Butternut Squash

If there is one vegetable that I love with my dal, it is squash. The creamy, sweet texture of the butternut squash makes the dal extra delicious. The crispy bits of garlic fried in ghee and the nigella seeds are the highlight of this dish. Nigella seeds are the black onion seeds used in Indian dishes for their subtle and sweet lingering aroma. In an Instant Pot, this butternut squash dal requires only six minutes of cooking. Isn't that perfect for a quick weeknight dinner?

SERVES 2

Vegetarian, Gluten Free

❄

Rinse the moong beans until the water runs clear. Soak them in water for 10 minutes.

Set the SAUTÉ mode of the Instant Pot for 10 minutes.

Add the oil to the inner pot. Once the oil is hot, add the nigella seeds, cumin seeds, garlic and onion to the pot. Sauté for 2 to 3 minutes, or until the onion is lightly browned.

Drain the water from the soaked moong beans, and transfer them to the Instant Pot along with the squash and green chile. Sauté for 2 minutes.

Add the water, salt, turmeric and red chili powder, and stir to combine. Close the lid. Set the steam valve to the sealing position. Pressure cook at high pressure for 6 minutes. Let the steam release manually.

Prepare the tempering: In a small skillet, heat the ghee over low to medium heat. Add the garlic and fry until lightly browned, 2 to 3 minutes. Pour this tempering over the dal.

Add the cilantro and drizzle with the lime juice (if using), and serve.

1 cup (200 g) dried yellow moong beans

2 tbsp (30 ml) vegetable oil

1 tsp nigella seeds

1 tsp cumin seeds

1 tsp chopped garlic

½ cup (80 g) finely chopped yellow onion

2 cups (280 g) peeled, seeded and cubed butternut squash

1 mild green chile, such as jalapeño, Thai green chile or serrano pepper, chopped

2 cups (480 ml) water

1 tsp salt

1 tsp ground turmeric

1 tsp red chili powder

1 tbsp (1 g) chopped fresh cilantro

1 tbsp (15 ml) fresh lime juice (optional)

TEMPERING (TADKA)

1 tbsp (14 g) ghee or coconut oil

1 tbsp (10 g) chopped garlic

Langar Wali Dal

Sikh Gurudwara-Style Lentil Curry

Serves 2

Vegan, Gluten Free

Langar **is the sacred food served at the community kitchen of a** ***gurudwara*****, the Sikh place of worship. This dal is a mix of black lentils, chickpeas and red kidney beans. The humble and comforting taste of** ***langar wali dal*** **is like a warm motherly hug. It is wholesome and nourishing. Instant Pot helped me perfectly re-create the gurudwara-style texture and taste of the dal at home. But if you have a chance to visit a gurudwara, try sampling the langar wali dal there and then you will understand the emotions behind it.**

- ½ cup (100 g) dried whole black lentils (sabut urad)
- ¼ cup (50 g) dried red kidney beans (rajma)
- ¼ cup (50 g) dried split chickpeas (chana dal)
- 2 tbsp (30 ml) vegetable oil
- 1 tsp cumin seeds
- ¼ tsp asafetida
- 1 tbsp (5 g) grated fresh ginger
- 1 cup (160 g) roughly chopped red onion
- ½ cup (90 g) chopped tomato
- ½ tsp ground turmeric
- ½ tsp red chili powder
- 2 tsp (12 g) salt
- 3 cups (720 ml) water, plus 1 to 2 tbsp (15 to 30 ml) if needed
- 1 tsp garam masala
- 1½ tsp (0.5 g) dried fenugreek leaves (kasuri methi)
- 2 mild green chiles, such as jalapeños, Thai green chiles or serrano peppers, thinly sliced or julienned
- 2 tbsp (2 g) chopped fresh cilantro

Combine the black lentils, red kidney beans and chickpeas, and rinse with water until the water runs clear. Soak them in water for 4 to 5 hours.

Set the SAUTÉ mode of the Instant Pot for 15 minutes. Add the oil to the inner pot. Once the oil is hot, add the cumin seeds, asafetida and ginger and sauté for 30 to 40 seconds. Add the red onion and fry until lightly browned, 5 to 6 minutes.

Add the tomato, turmeric, red chili powder and salt; fry the masala until the tomato is mashed nicely and oil starts oozing from the sides, 2 to 3 minutes. If the masala is burning or sticking to the pot, add 1 to 2 tablespoons (15 to 30 ml) of water and stir.

Drain all the water from the soaked legumes. Add them to the Instant Pot and sauté with the masala until the timer beeps.

Add the 3 cups (720 ml) of water and give the dal a good stir. Close the lid of the Instant Pot. Set the steam valve to the sealing position. Pressure cook at the normal setting for 30 minutes.

Once the timer beeps, let the steam release naturally. Open the lid. Check the dal for doneness—it should be soft and fully cooked.

Add the garam masala, fenugreek leaves, green chiles and cilantro. Stir to combine.

Set the SAUTÉ mode for 5 minutes to simmer and thicken the dal before serving.

Serve with rice and roti for a hearty gurudwara-style meal.

Note:

- **Alternatively, you can slow cook this dal. Simply follow the recipe as written, but instead of pressure cooking the dal for 30 minutes, set your Instant Pot to SLOW COOK mode for 5 hours or overnight.**

SABUT MASOOR DAL

Brown Lentil Curry with Spinach and Potatoes

The brown lentil is one of the most readily available lentils, as well as a humble, utterly delicious and easy-to-cook legume. In India, it is known as *sabut masoor dal, sabut* meaning "whole." You can transform this plain-looking lentil in a million creative ways, from stew to curry. This is a comforting, nourishing curry that pairs brown lentils with fresh spinach and potato. With a side of any type of Indian bread, it is one of my favorite comforting, weeknight dinners.

SERVES 2

Vegetarian, Gluten Free

Rinse the lentils until the water runs clear. Soak them in water for 15 minutes.

Set the SAUTÉ mode of the Instant Pot for 6 minutes.

Add the ghee to the inner pot. Once the ghee is hot, add the cumin seeds and ginger. Sauté until the aroma of ginger is released, 20 to 30 seconds.

Next, add the onion and fry, stirring to prevent it from burning, for 1 to 2 minutes, or until lightly browned.

Add the potato, turmeric, red chili powder and salt, and mix nicely.

Drain all the water from the soaked lentils. Add them to the inner pot. Fry for a minute while stirring at regular intervals.

Add the spinach and water, and stir. Taste, and add more salt or seasoning, if needed.

Close the lid. Set the steam valve to the sealing position. Pressure cook at high pressure for 10 minutes.

After the timer beeps, let the steam release naturally.

Open the lid, add the garam masala, cilantro, lemon juice and butter (if using), and stir to combine.

Serve with rice or your flatbread of choice.

1 cup (200 g) dried brown lentils (whole masoor dal)

4 tbsp (55 g) ghee or unsalted butter

1 tsp cumin seeds

1 tbsp (5 g) grated fresh ginger

½ cup (80 g) finely chopped yellow onion

1 cup (170 g) peeled and diced potato

¼ tsp ground turmeric

½ tsp red chili powder or paprika

1½ tsp (9 g) salt, or to taste

1 cup (30 g) baby spinach leaves or chopped spinach

2 cups (480 ml) water

1 tsp garam masala

2 tbsp (2 g) chopped fresh cilantro

Fresh lemon juice, to taste

1 tbsp (14 g) unsalted butter (optional; see note)

NOTE:

❋ You can add a tablespoon (14 g) of butter before serving the dal, for an extra-rich, buttery flavor.

SOUTH INDIA SPECIAL SAMBAR

Pigeon Peas and Vegetable Stew

Sambar is the flag bearer of South Indian cuisine: a sweet, spicy, sour stew of lentils, vegetables and spices. Whether it is a plate of *idli* (steamed fermented rice and lentil cakes), crispy *dosa* (Indian crepe) or a typical South Indian food, it's all incomplete without a bowl of sambar. The best part of a sambar is you can customize it by adding vegetables of your choice. I like to add drumsticks to the sambar—but not the chicken variety. In fact, it is a vegetable that grows as the stem of moringa plant—the New Age superfood from India well known for its immunity-boosting benefits.

1 cup (170 g) dried split pigeon peas (toor dal)

4 tbsp (55 g) ghee

½ cup (80 g) chopped shallots or onion

4 cloves garlic, chopped

½ cup (90 g) chopped tomato

¼ cup (33 g) peeled and diced carrot

⅓ cup (47 g) peeled and diced bottle gourd (calabash)

6 to 8 pieces drumstick, cleaned and peeled

2 tsp (4 g) ground turmeric

1 tsp red chili powder

2 tsp (12 g) salt

3 cups (720 ml) water

2 tbsp (30 g) dark brown sugar or jaggery powder

1 tbsp (15 g) tamarind paste

1 tbsp (6 g) sambar masala (optional; see note)

TEMPERING (TADKA)

2 tbsp (28 g) ghee

1½ tsp (6 g) black mustard seeds (rai)

¼ tsp asafetida

6 to 8 curry leaves

2 dried red chiles, such as Kashmiri

Rinse the pigeon peas until the water runs clear. Soak them in water for 10 minutes.

Set the SAUTÉ mode of the Instant Pot for 6 minutes. Add the ghee to the inner pot. Once the ghee is hot, add the shallots and garlic. Sauté for 1 to 2 minutes, or until they turn translucent.

Next, drain all the water from the soaked pigeon peas. Add them to the inner pot. Sauté for 1 minute. Add the tomato, carrot, bottle gourd, drumstick, turmeric, red chili powder and salt, and sauté until the timer beeps.

Add the water. Stir the sambar. Close the lid. Set the steam valve to the sealing position. Pressure cook at high pressure for 15 minutes. Once the timer beeps, let the steam release naturally. Open the lid.

Prepare the tempering: In a small skillet, heat the ghee over medium heat. Add the mustard seeds, asafetida, curry leaves and red chiles, and fry for 2 to 3 minutes. Pour this tempering over the sambar in the Instant Pot. Add the brown sugar, tamarind paste and sambar masala, and stir to combine.

Set the SAUTÉ mode for 5 minutes to simmer the sambar.

Serve with idli and dosa.

NOTE:

✷ Do not get intimidated by the mention of sambar masala—it is a simple spice blend and easily available at Indian grocery stores. It gives an authentic taste to the dish.

KADALA CURRY

Brown Chickpea and Potato Masala

My favorite vegetarian dish from the Indian state of Kerala is *kadala curry*, a subtle spicy curry of brown chickpeas with coconut and whole spices. I like to add potatoes to make it more delicious and comforting. Brown chickpeas are a bit smaller than white chickpeas, with light brown skin and are used in a variety of Indian curries for their nutty flavor and starchy texture.

SERVES 2

Vegan, Gluten Free

❖

Rinse the chickpeas until the water runs clear. Soak them in water for 5 to 6 hours or overnight.

Prepare the masala paste: Set the SAUTÉ mode of the Instant Pot for 15 minutes.

In the inner pot, combine the coconut oil, desiccated coconut, green chile, garlic, cilantro stalks and peppercorns. Sauté for 1 minute to release the aroma. Transfer the mixture to a blender, add the tablespoon (15 ml) of water and blend into a coarse paste. Set aside.

Prepare the curry: Add the coconut oil to the rinsed inner pot of the Instant Pot.

Next, add the cinnamon stick, cardamom pods, mustard seeds, curry leaves and dried red chiles. Sauté for 20 to 30 seconds, or until the seeds start to splutter.

Add the onion and fry for 3 to 5 minutes, or until lightly golden.

Add the tomato, turmeric, red chili powder, salt and coriander, and sauté the masala until the tomato is soft, about 3 minutes.

Drain all the water from the soaked chickpeas. Add them to the Instant Pot and stir to combine with the masala. Add the water and give the curry a good stir.

Close the lid. Set the steam valve to the sealing position. Pressure cook at high pressure for 20 minutes. Once the timer beeps, let the steam release naturally.

Open the lid. Add the potatoes (see note), the prepared curry masala paste and the garam masala, and stir to combine. Add more salt, if needed, at this stage.

Close the lid. Set the steam valve to the sealing position. Pressure cook at high pressure for 10 minutes. Do a quick release of steam.

Serve with your flatbread of choice or rice.

NOTE:

❖ Cooking potatoes for 30 minutes is not recommended, as they will fall apart.

1 cup (200 g) dried brown chickpeas (chana)

MASALA PASTE

1 tsp coconut oil

¼ cup (21 g) desiccated coconut

1 mild green chile, such as jalapeño, Thai green chile or serrano peppers, chopped

4 cloves garlic

1 tbsp (1 g) chopped cilantro stalks

½ tsp black peppercorns

1 tbsp (15 ml) water (see note)

CURRY

4 tbsp (55 g) coconut oil

1 (1" [2.5-cm])-long piece cinnamon stick

4 green cardamom pods

1 tsp black mustard seeds

5 to 6 curry leaves

2 dried red chiles, such as Kashmiri

½ cup (80 g) finely chopped yellow onion

½ cup (90 g) roughly chopped tomato

½ tsp ground turmeric

¼ tsp red chili powder or paprika

1 tsp salt

1 tsp ground coriander

2 cups (480 ml) water

1 cup (170 g) whole baby potatoes (see note)

1 tsp garam masala

SAAG MAA KI DAL

Green Leafy Lentil Curry

Saag maa ki dal is a delectable vegetarian combination of green leafy vegetables, such as mustard, spinach and fenugreek, with two kinds of legumes. A lost rustic recipe from the rural northern province of India, it was mainly developed for the farmers working hard in the fields throughout the day. This dish is rich, creamy and nourishing. You can use a combination of mustard greens, spinach and kale, or only spinach or kale, to make this dal.

½ cup (90 g) dried split black lentils (chilka urad dal)

¼ cup (50 g) dried split chickpeas (chana dal)

2 cups (134 g) finely chopped mustard leaves (sarson)

1 cup (67 g) chopped curly kale

1 cup (30 g) baby spinach

1 mild green chile, such as jalapeño, Thai green chile or serrano pepper, finely chopped

1 tsp salt

¼ tsp ground turmeric

1 tbsp (5 g) finely chopped fresh ginger

1½ cups (360 ml) water, divided

2 tbsp (18 g) cornmeal

TEMPERING (TADKA)

4 tbsp (55 g) ghee

1 tsp cumin seeds

¼ tsp asafetida

2 tbsp (10 g) sliced garlic

2 dried red chiles, such as Kashmiri, broken

1 tsp red chili powder (optional)

Rinse the black lentils and chickpeas until the water runs clear. Soak the lentils in water for 5 to 6 hours; soak the split chickpeas separately for only 10 minutes.

After the black lentils' soak time is up, gently rub them to get rid of any loosely floating black peel or skin. Drain all the water from both the lentils and chickpeas and set them aside.

In the inner pot of the Instant Pot, combine the mustard leaves, kale, spinach, green chile, salt, turmeric and ginger. Mix nicely. Add ¼ cup (60 ml) of the water.

Close the lid. Set the steam valve to the sealing position. Pressure cook at high pressure for 2 minutes. Let the steam release naturally. Open the lid. Gently mash the green leaves, using the back of the ladle or a potato masher.

Add the drained legumes and 1 cup (240 ml) of the water, stir to combine and close the lid of the Instant Pot. Set the steam valve to the sealing position. Pressure cook at high pressure for 25 minutes. Once the cooking time is over, wait for the natural release. Open the lid, and gently mash the dal, using the back of the ladle.

Set the SAUTÉ mode for 5 minutes.

Meanwhile, in a small bowl, combine the cornmeal with the remaining ¼ cup (60 ml) of water to form a smooth slurry or paste. Add it to the dal and stir to combine. This gives the dal a luscious texture and taste.

Prepare the tempering: In a skillet, heat the ghee over medium heat. Add the cumin, asafetida, garlic, red chiles and red chili powder, if using. Fry until the garlic becomes lightly browned. Pour this tadka over the dal. Stir to combine. Let the dal sit in the Instant Pot for 5 minutes, covered, before serving.

Serve with naan or chapati.

Vegetable Chana Curry

Vegan Chickpea Coconut Curry

SERVES 2

Vegan, Gluten Free

Chickpeas (white chana) are an excellent source of plant-based protein. In Indian cuisine, they are commonly used to make a variety of curries and other dishes. This is a typical modern-day creamy chickpea curry packed with vegetables and flavored with coconut milk—a wholesome, fulfilling curry perfect for the weeknight family dinner.

Prepare the paste: In a blender or food processor, blend the tomato, red chiles and ginger into a smooth paste. Set aside.

Prepare the curry: Transfer the canned chickpeas to a colander. Rinse them with water to get rid of the starch and sodium. Let them sit in the colander until you're ready to use them.

Set the SAUTÉ mode of the Instant Pot for 10 minutes.

Add the oil to the inner pot. Add the cinnamon stick, nigella seeds and cumin seeds, and fry for 20 to 30 seconds.

Add the red onion and fry for 3 minutes, or until the onion is lightly browned.

Next, add the prepared masala paste, turmeric, paprika and salt, and sauté for 2 to 3 minutes. Add the potato, carrot and drained chickpeas, and stir to combine.

Add the water, mix, then close the lid. Set the steam valve to the sealing position. Pressure cook at high pressure for 5 minutes. Let the steam release naturally.

Open the lid. Add the coconut milk, spinach and garam masala. Stir to mix. Set the SAUTÉ mode for 5 minutes to simmer the curry.

The curry is ready to serve!

PASTE

½ cup (90 g) roughly chopped tomato

2 dried red chiles, such as Kashmiri, or to taste

1 tbsp (5 g) chopped fresh ginger

CURRY

1 cup (240 g) canned chickpeas

4 tbsp (55 g) coconut oil

1 (½" [1.3-cm])-long piece cinnamon stick

1 tsp nigella seeds

1 tsp cumin seeds

½ cup (80 g) finely chopped red onion

1 tsp ground turmeric

1 tsp paprika

2 tsp (12 g) salt

½ cup (85 g) peeled and diced potato

½ cup (65 g) peeled and diced carrot

1¼ cups (300 ml) water

¼ cup (60 ml) coconut milk

1 cup (30 g) baby spinach

½ tsp garam masala

SERVES 2

Vegetarian, Gluten Free

❈

SQUASH METHI DAL

Winter Squash, Fenugreek and Pink Lentil Curry

Squash and pink lentils, a.k.a. *masoor dal*, are a match made in heaven. This dal is hearty and full of flavors, packed with the sweetness of winter squash, the bitterness of fresh fenugreek leaves, the sourness of tamarind, the creaminess of coconut milk and the spiciness of chiles—making it perfectly umami.

1¼ cups (225 g) dried whole pink lentils (masoor dal)

4 tbsp (55 g) ghee

1 tsp black mustard seeds

1 tsp cumin seeds

5 to 6 curry leaves

2 dried red chiles, such as Kashmiri

1 tbsp (5 g) grated fresh ginger

½ cup (80 g) finely chopped yellow onion

1 cup (140 g) peeled, cubed, and seeded winter squash

1 cup (55 g) chopped fresh fenugreek leaves

1 tbsp (15 g) tamarind paste (see note)

1 tsp red chili powder

½ tsp ground turmeric

1 tsp salt

1 tsp light brown sugar or jaggery powder

2 cups (480 ml) water

1 tbsp (15 ml) coconut cream

1 tsp garam masala

1 tbsp (1 g) chopped fresh cilantro

Rinse the lentils until the water runs clear. Soak them in water until you're ready to use them.

Set the SAUTÉ mode of the Instant Pot for 10 minutes.

Add the ghee to the inner pot. Add the mustard seeds, cumin seeds, curry leaves, red chiles and ginger, and sauté for 20 seconds, or until the seeds start to splutter.

Add the onion and fry for 3 minutes, or until lightly browned.

Drain the water from the soaked lentils. Add the lentils to the inner pot along with the squash and fenugreek leaves. Sauté for 1 minute.

Add the tamarind paste, red chili powder, turmeric, salt, brown sugar and water. Mix nicely.

Close the lid. Set the steam valve to the sealing position. Pressure cook at the normal pressure setting for 5 minutes. Wait for the natural release of steam.

Open the lid. Add the coconut cream, garam masala and cilantro. Stir to combine.

Serve warm.

NOTE:

❈ Alternatively, for sourness, you can replace the tamarind paste with an equal amount of lime juice. Add it while adding coconut cream, toward the end, and not while pressure cooking.

VEGETABLE KOOTU

Vegetable and Yellow Moong Bean Curry

Kootu is a Tamil word, meaning "to add." Vegetable kootu is another popular vegetarian stew from the southern region of India. Flavored with coconut milk, it contains moong beans and a medley of mixed seasonal vegetables. The PRESSURE COOK mode of the Instant Pot is ideal to make a perfectly creamy, thick kootu just the way Grandma would make it. You can use any combination of mixed vegetables for this dal recipe. Make sure to pick vegetables that do not take a long time to cook.

Rinse the yellow moong beans until the water runs clear. Soak them in water until you're ready to use them.

Set the SAUTÉ mode of the Instant Pot for 8 minutes.

Add the oil to the inner pot. Add the mustard seeds, cumin seeds, curry leaves and skinned black gram lentil, and sauté for 20 seconds, or until the seeds start to splutter.

Add the red onion and fry for 3 minutes, or until lightly browned.

Drain the water from the soaked moong beans. Add to the inner pot along with the mixed vegetables. Sauté for 1 minute.

Season with the salt, turmeric and red chili powder. Stir to combine.

Add the water and stir. Close the lid. Set the steam valve to the sealing position. Pressure cook at high pressure for 6 minutes, then use a quick manual release.

Open the lid. Add the coconut milk. Stir to combine. Set the SAUTÉ mode and simmer the curry for 2 to 3 minutes.

Serve with chapati or dosa for a wholesome meal.

½ cup (100 g) dried yellow moong beans

4 tbsp (60 ml) refined oil, such as vegetable oil

1 tsp black mustard seeds

1 tsp cumin seeds

5 to 6 curry leaves

1 tsp skinned black gram lentil (urad dal)

1 cup (160 g) sliced red onion

1 cup (125 g) mixed vegetables (peas, carrot, beans, cauliflower)

1 tsp salt

1 tsp ground turmeric

1 tsp red chili powder

1¼ cups (300 ml) water

¼ cup (60 ml) thick coconut milk

SQUASH RED BEANS CURRY

Red Kidney Beans and Winter Squash Curry

Rich red beans and the soft texture of winter squash complement each other perfectly in a creamy South Indian–style curry. This unique ingredient combination is one you won't find in a restaurant! It's a perfect protein- and fiber-packed vegan curry that will add variety to your Instant Pot repertoire.

1½ cups (300 g) dried red kidney beans (rajma; see notes)

¼ cup (25 g) desiccated coconut

4 cloves garlic

¼ tsp cumin seeds

2 dried red chiles, such as Kashmiri, broken in half

2 cups (480 ml) water, plus 1 to 2 tbsp (15 to 30 ml) if needed (see notes)

4 tbsp (60 ml) coconut oil

1 tsp black mustard seeds (rai)

5 to 6 fresh curry leaves

½ cup (80 g) finely chopped yellow onion

1½ tsp (9 g) salt, or to taste

1 tsp ground turmeric

1 tsp red chili powder (optional)

1 cup (140 g) peeled, seeded and diced winter squash

1 tbsp (1 g) finely chopped fresh cilantro, for garnish

Rinse the red kidney beans until the water runs clear. Soak them in enough water to cover for 4 to 5 hours or overnight.

In a blender or food processor, blend the coconut, garlic, cumin seeds and dried red chiles to a coarse paste. If needed, use 1 to 2 tablespoons (15 to 30 ml) of the water to process the ingredients. Set this masala aside to use later.

Set the SAUTÉ mode of the Instant Pot for 5 minutes.

Add the oil to the inner pot. Once the oil is hot, add the mustard seeds and curry leaves, and stir. Once the seeds start to pop, add the onion. Fry the onion, stirring to prevent it from burning, for 3 to 4 minutes, or until it is lightly browned.

Drain all the water from the soaked kidney beans. Add the beans to the inner pot.

Add the salt, turmeric and red chili powder, and sauté until the timer beeps.

Add the water and stir to combine.

Close the lid. Set the steam valve to the sealing position. Pressure cook at high pressure for 20 minutes. The cooking time may vary according to the variety of red beans.

After 20 minutes, let the steam release naturally. Open the lid. Check the beans for doneness. If they are soft and fully cooked through, add the diced squash and ground masala, and mix nicely.

Close the lid. Set the steam valve to the sealing position. Pressure cook at high pressure for 5 minutes. Use a quick release of steam.

Garnish with cilantro. Serve with cooked white or brown rice.

NOTES:

❋ You can replace the 2 cups (480 ml) of water with 2 cups (480 ml) of coconut milk for a delicious creamy taste.

❋ If you are using canned beans, there is no need to cook the squash and beans separately. A one-time 5 minutes of pressure cooking is good enough.

Palak Lobia Masala

Spinach and Black-Eyed Peas Curry

In India, black-eyed peas are known as *lobia*. They are commonly used to make a variety of curries. One of my favorite combinations is a spicy black-eyed peas curry flavored with spinach and loads of garlic, all cooked in an Instant Pot. This is a comforting, warming and easy-to-make curry that will make you fall in love with black-eyed peas.

SERVES 2

Vegetarian, Gluten Free

Rinse the black-eyed peas until the water runs clear. Soak them in enough water to cover for 4 to 5 hours or overnight.

Set the SAUTÉ mode of the Instant Pot for 5 minutes. Add 1 cup (240 ml) of water. Once the water starts to boil, add the spinach. Cook for 1 minute. Transfer the spinach to a bowl filled with cold water. Discard the hot water in the Instant Pot. Drain and transfer the blanched spinach to a blender, then add the green chiles and ginger and blend into a smooth puree. Set aside.

Set the SAUTÉ mode of the Instant Pot for 10 minutes. Add the ghee to the inner pot. Once the ghee is hot, add the garlic and sauté for 1 minute, or until it is lightly golden.

Add the red onion. Fry for 3 to 4 minutes, or until the onion is lightly browned.

Next, add the tomato, salt, turmeric and red chili powder. Stir to mix. Sauté for 2 minutes, or until the tomato breaks down completely.

Drain all the water from the soaked black-eyed peas. Add them to the inner pot. Sauté for 2 minutes. Add the remaining 1½ cups (360 ml) of water and stir to mix. Close the lid. Set the steam valve to the sealing position. Pressure cook at high pressure for 20 minutes. Wait for the natural release of the steam.

Open the lid. Add the spinach puree and garam masala, and stir to combine. Simmer the curry in SAUTÉ mode for 5 minutes. Serve warm.

1 cup (200 g) dried black-eyed peas (lobia)

2½ cups (600 ml) water, divided

2 cups (60 g) spinach leaves, chopped

2 mild green chiles, such as jalapeños, Thai green chiles or serrano peppers, chopped

1 tbsp (5 g) chopped fresh ginger

4 tbsp (55 g) ghee

2 tbsp (10 g) finely chopped garlic

1 cup (160 g) finely chopped red onion

½ cup (90 g) finely chopped tomato

2 tsp (12 g) salt

1 tsp ground turmeric

1 tsp red chili powder

1 tsp garam masala

VEG CURRY IN A HURRY

Vegetable curries are the essence of Indian cuisine, and in this chapter, you will find unique, delicious-to-the-core vegetarian curries that are far from boring. From the time of the Indus Valley and Harappan civilization, the people of the Indian subcontinent have been farmers. And as time passed, so did the spread of such religions as Jainism, Buddhism and Hinduism—along with their firm beliefs of nonviolence and vegetarianism.

I am happy that the love for vegetarianism is growing firm. It is no longer considered an unconventional choice by food lovers and is appreciated by some top chefs and Michelin-starred restaurants.

Today, India is at the top ranking when it comes to having a purely vegetarian population. The variety of vegetables available and the curries created with them can help you plan the menu for 365 days without repeating a single curry. Contrary to popular belief, in India, vegetable curry is called *sabzi* or *tarkari*, not *curry*.

There are curries made with a combination of seasonal vegetables, such as Mix Veg Masala (page 88). A few are made by cooking legumes and vegetables together. At the same time, a few have vegetarian protein, such as paneer, tofu or soy curls as the core ingredient. And then we have vegetable stews, such as Kale Boondi Kadhi (page 91).

This chapter is dedicated to my favorite vegetable curries that are ready in under 30 minutes in an Instant Pot. These pure vegetarian curries are wholesome, easy to cook, truly delicious and more important, thanks to the Instant Pot, you do not have to spend hours in the kitchen to cook a single meal. Writing this chapter has made me fall in love with vegetarian curries and reminded me of their simple yet delicious taste.

MUSHROOM MATAR MASALA

Spicy Button Mushroom and Green Peas Curry

In the last 50 years in India, button mushrooms have become one of the most popular "functional foods" and a great alternative to meat with regard to nutritional value. The reason for its popularity is the chewy, fibrous texture similar to meat. Hence, for the pure vegetarians like my mother, it adds a great variety to main courses. This delicious button mushroom and green peas curry in a spicy, creamy masala paste pull together effortlessly in an Instant Pot in under 30 minutes.

4 tbsp (60 ml) cooking oil

1 bay leaf

1 cup (160 g) finely chopped white onion

1 tbsp (20 g) ginger and garlic paste

½ cup (122 g) canned crushed tomato

1 tsp red chili powder or paprika

1 tsp ground turmeric

1 tsp salt

¼ cup (60 ml) water, plus 1 to 2 tbsp (15 to 30 ml) if needed

2 cups (140 g) diced button mushrooms

½ cup (75 g) green peas, fresh or frozen

4 tbsp (60 ml) light cream (see note)

1 tsp garam masala

1 tbsp (1 g) dried fenugreek leaves (kasuri methi)

2 tbsp (2 g) chopped fresh cilantro, for garnish

Set the SAUTÉ mode of the Instant Pot for 10 minutes.

Add the oil to the inner pot. Once the oil is hot, add the bay leaf and onion. Sauté for 3 to 4 minutes, or until the onion is lightly browned.

Add the ginger and garlic paste, mix well, and cook for 1 minute. Add the tomato, red chili powder, turmeric and salt. Sauté the masala until it starts to leave the sides of the pot, 2 to 3 minutes. If the masala is sticking to the pot, add 1 to 2 tablespoons (15 to 30 ml) of water.

Add the mushrooms and green peas, and sauté until the timer beeps.

Add the ¼ cup (60 ml) of water and stir. Close the lid. Set the steam valve to the sealing position. Pressure cook for 5 minutes at the normal pressure setting.

After 5 minutes, set the steam valve to the venting position. Open the lid of the Instant Pot. Add the cream, garam masala and fenugreek leaves.

Set the SAUTÉ mode for 5 minutes to thicken the curry sauce a bit, stirring regularly to prevent burning the curry. Remove and discard the bay leaf before serving.

Garnish with the cilantro. Serve with naan or jeera rice.

NOTE:

❃ To make vegan mushroom masala, use cashew cream or coconut milk instead of light cream.

Squash Potato Curry

Sweet and Spicy Winter Squash Potato Curry

The holy cities of India, such as Mathura and Benares, are known for their rich culture and cuisine. The spiritual significance of these cities also impacts the cuisine of the region, which is mainly *sattvic*, rich in dairy and revolves around fresh produce. This sweet, spicy, simple squash curry is a popular main course dish served with piping hot fried bread (poori) in every home, nook and corner of northern and central India. The Hindi name of this dish is *bhandara wali aloo kaddu ki sabzi*.

Prepare the masala paste: In a blender, blend the tomato and ginger into a smooth paste. Set aside.

Set the SAUTÉ mode of the Instant Pot for 8 minutes.

Add the oil to the inner pot. Once the oil is smoking hot, add the mustard seeds, cumin seeds, asafetida, fenugreek seeds and red chiles, and sauté for 20 minutes, or until the seeds start to splutter.

Add the masala paste, red chili powder, turmeric, coriander and salt, and sauté until the masala comes together nicely or the oil starts oozing from the masala, 2 to 3 minutes.

Add the potato and squash, and sauté until the timer beeps.

Add the water and close the lid. Set the steam valve to the sealing position. Pressure cook at high pressure for 5 minutes. Let the steam release naturally.

Gently mash the curry with the back of a ladle to thicken the gravy. Add the fenugreek leaves and cilantro.

Serve with poori or paratha.

SERVES 2

Vegan, Gluten Free

✥

Masala Paste

1 cup (180 g) chopped tomato

1 tbsp (5 g) chopped fresh ginger

Curry

4 tbsp (60 ml) mustard oil or (55 g) ghee

1 tsp black mustard seeds

1 tsp cumin seeds

¼ tsp asafetida

¼ tsp fenugreek seeds

2 dried red chiles, such as Kashmiri

1 tsp red chili powder

1 tsp ground turmeric

½ tsp ground coriander

1¼ tsp (7 g) salt

1 cup (170 g) peeled and diced potato

1 cup (140 g) peeled, diced and seeded winter squash

1½ cups (360 ml) water

1 tsp dried fenugreek leaves (kasuri methi)

2 tbsp (2 g) chopped fresh cilantro leaves

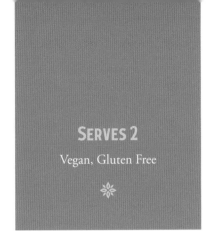

PASTE

¼ cup (20 g) chopped coconut

1 tbsp (5 g) chopped fresh ginger

2 mild green chiles, such as jalapeños, Thai green chiles or serrano peppers, chopped

¼ cup (4 g) chopped fresh cilantro stalks

1 tbsp (15 ml) water

CURRY

4 tbsp (55 g) coconut oil

1 tsp mustard seeds

5 to 6 curry leaves

1 cup (160 g) shallots (sambar onion)

2 cups (280 g) diced pineapple (see note)

1 tsp salt

½ tsp ground turmeric

½ tsp red chili powder

1 tbsp (15 g) light brown sugar

1 cup (240 ml) water

1 tsp sambar masala or curry powder

1 tbsp (1 g) chopped fresh cilantro, for garnish

SOUTH INDIAN–STYLE PINEAPPLE CURRY

Vegan Pineapple Curry

Like tomato and green chile, pineapple also entered Indian kitchens relatively recently. Over the years, it became highly popular in the southern and coastal regions of India. From fresh juices, sweets, pudding and raita to curry, pineapple is used profusely in the southern states. This pineapple curry is a perfect umami with a balance of sweet, spicy, salty and tart. It tastes finger-licking good with steamed rice and fried papadum. And the PRESSURE COOK mode of an Instant Pot cooks the pineapple to perfection, making the curry all the more delicious.

Prepare the paste: In a blender or food processor, blend the coconut, ginger, green chile, cilantro and water to a smooth paste. Set aside until you're ready to use it.

Set the SAUTÉ mode of the Instant Pot for 6 minutes.

Add the oil to the inner pot. Once the oil is hot, add the mustard seeds, curry leaves and shallots. Sauté until the shallots are tender and translucent, 2 to 3 minutes.

Add the pineapple cubes, salt, turmeric, red chili powder and brown sugar. Sauté for 2 to 3 minutes.

Add the blended masala paste, water and sambar masala, and stir to combine.

Close the lid. Set the steam valve to the sealing position. Pressure cook at high pressure for 8 minutes. Wait for the natural release of steam.

Garnish with the cilantro. Serve with rice.

NOTE:

✴ The pressure cook time may vary according to the variety of the pineapple. It is best to select sweet, ripe and firm pineapple for this curry recipe.

TOFU MATAR MASALA

Peas and Tofu Curry

SERVES 2

Vegan, Gluten Free

For the nation that is obsessed with paneer, *matar paneer* is one of the most loved curries. Every family has its own take on this famous Indian curry. This recipe is my vegan version of it. Soft, melt-in-your-mouth cubes of tofu cooked with green peas in a spicy gravy of tomato and onion—what is there not to love?

Set the SAUTÉ mode of the Instant Pot for 8 minutes.

Add the oil to the inner pot. Once the oil is hot, add the bay leaf and cumin seeds. Sauté for 20 to 30 seconds. Add the onion and fry for 3 minutes, or until lightly browned.

Add the ginger and garlic paste. Sauté for 40 to 50 seconds, or until the raw smell wafts away.

Add the tomato, turmeric, coriander, red chili powder and salt, and fry the masala for 2 to 3 minutes. Add the roasted gram flour and fry the masala for another minute.

Add the water, tofu and peas, and stir. Close the lid. Set the steam valve to the sealing position. Pressure cook at high pressure for 5 minutes. Release the pressure manually. Remove and discard the bay leaf before serving.

Add the green chiles and cilantro, and serve warm.

NOTE:

❋ A firm, packed block of tofu is the best choice for this curry, not silken tofu. If it need not be vegan, you can use paneer instead of tofu.

4 tbsp (60 ml) mustard oil

1 bay leaf

1 tsp cumin seeds

1 cup (160 g) yellow onion, finely chopped

1 tbsp (20 g) ginger and garlic paste

1 cup (244 g) canned crushed tomato

1 tsp ground turmeric

1 tsp ground coriander

1 tsp Kashmiri red chili powder

1¼ tsp (7 g) salt

1 tbsp (8 g) roasted gram (chickpea) flour

1½ cups (360 ml) water

1½ cups (345 g) cubed firm tofu (see note)

1 cup (150 g) green peas, fresh or frozen

2 mild green chiles, such as jalapeños, Thai green chiles or serrano peppers, sliced

2 tbsp (2 g) chopped fresh cilantro

CREAMY CAULIFLOWER PEAS CURRY

Coconut-Flavored Cauliflower and Peas Curry

This one-pot wonder curry makes an excellent weeknight dinner with naan or steamed basmati rice. The coconut milk does a fantastic job of making the curry saucy and delicious. The addition of turmeric gives a golden color to the curry. All you need are a few basic Indian pantry staples and an Instant Pot to make this family-friendly curry at home.

4 tbsp (55 g) coconut oil

1 tsp nigella seeds

1 tbsp (5 g) grated fresh ginger

½ cup (80 g) yellow onion, finely chopped

¼ cup (61 g) canned crushed tomato

1¼ tsp (7 g) salt

¼ tsp red chili powder

1 tsp ground turmeric

½ tsp freshly ground black pepper

2 cups (200 g) cauliflower florets

½ cup (75 g) green peas, fresh or frozen

1 cup (170 g) peeled and diced potato

¼ cup (60 ml) water

½ cup (120 ml) thick coconut milk

2 tbsp (2 g) chopped fresh cilantro, for garnish

Set the SAUTÉ mode of the Instant Pot for 10 minutes.

Add the oil to the inner pot. Once the oil is hot, add the nigella seeds and ginger, and fry for 10 to 20 seconds.

Add the onion. Sauté for 3 to 4 minutes, or until lightly browned.

Add the tomato, salt, red chili powder, turmeric and black pepper, and sauté for 2 to 3 minutes.

Add the cauliflower, green peas, potato and water, and stir to combine. Taste and add more seasoning, if needed.

Close the lid. Set the steam valve to the sealing position. Pressure cook at high pressure for 3 minutes. Wait for the natural release of steam.

Open the lid of the Instant Pot. Add the coconut milk and stir to combine. Simmer the curry in SAUTÉ mode for 5 minutes.

Serve garnished with the cilantro.

Zucchini Kofta Curry

Vegetarian Kofta Balls Curry

This vegan *kofta* recipe will make you fall in love with zucchini. The kofta are crisp and moist, and taste so good when dunked in a flavorsome curry. For frying kofta, you can use the SAUTÉ mode, or the Instant Pot accessories for air frying if you have them. I've included instructions for both methods.

Prepare the kofta: In a large bowl, combine the zucchini and salt. Set aside for 15 minutes for the squash to release all its liquid. Once the liquid is released, squeeze the zucchini tightly in small batches to drain out all the water.

Transfer the squeezed-out zucchini to a separate large bowl. Add the gram flour, rice flour, turmeric and red chili powder. Mix nicely. Take 1 tablespoon (17 g) of the kofta mixture and form a round, flat patty ½ inch (1.3 cm) thick. Similarly shape all of the kofta. Refrigerate them until ready to fry.

To air fry: Assemble the Instant Pot air fryer basket. Spray it with cooking spray. Arrange the kofta neatly in the basket. Set the AIR FRY mode and cook until the kofta are crisp from the outside and fully cooked inside, turning them halfway through cooking. This should take 10 minutes in total (5 minutes on each side).

To sauté: Set the SAUTÉ mode of the Instant Pot for 10 minutes. Add the oil to the inner pot. Once hot, add the kofta and cook until crisp on both sides.

Prepare the onion paste: In a blender, blend the onion, ginger, garlic and green chile to a smooth paste. Use 1 to 2 tablespoons (15 to 30 ml) of water, if needed.

Prepare the curry sauce: Set the SAUTÉ mode for 10 minutes.

Add the oil to the inner pot. Once the oil is hot, add the cumin seeds and onion paste. Sauté for 2 to 3 minutes.

Add the tomato, turmeric, red chili powder, coriander and salt. Fry the masala until the timer beeps.

Add the water and stir to combine. Close the lid. Cook in SOUP mode for 5 minutes. Wait for the natural release of steam.

Add the coconut cream, garam masala and fenugreek leaves, and simmer the curry in SAUTÉ mode for 5 minutes.

Once the curry starts to simmer, gently add the cooked kofta and let them simmer in the sauce until the timer beeps. Do not simmer the kofta in the curry sauce for too long as they might break apart; 2 to 3 minutes of simmering time is fine. Garnish with the cilantro and serve!

KOFTA

4 cups (480 g) grated zucchini

1 tsp salt

1 cup (120 g) gram (chickpea) flour

¼ cup (40 g) rice flour

1 tsp ground turmeric

½ tsp red chili powder

Cooking spray (if air frying)

4 tbsp (60 ml) oil (if sautéing)

ONION PASTE

1 cup (160 g) chopped yellow onion

1 tbsp (5 g) chopped fresh ginger

1 tbsp (10 g) chopped garlic

1 mild green chile, such as jalapeño, Thai green chile or serrano pepper, chopped

1 to 2 tbsp (15 to 30 ml) water, if needed

CURRY SAUCE

4 tbsp (60 ml) oil

1 tsp cumin seeds

¼ cup (61 g) canned crushed tomato

½ tsp ground turmeric

½ tsp red chili powder

½ tsp ground coriander

1 tsp salt

1 cup (240 ml) water

2 tbsp (30 ml) coconut cream

1 tsp garam masala

1 tsp dried fenugreek leaves (kasuri methi)

2 tbsp (2 g) chopped fresh cilantro, for garnish

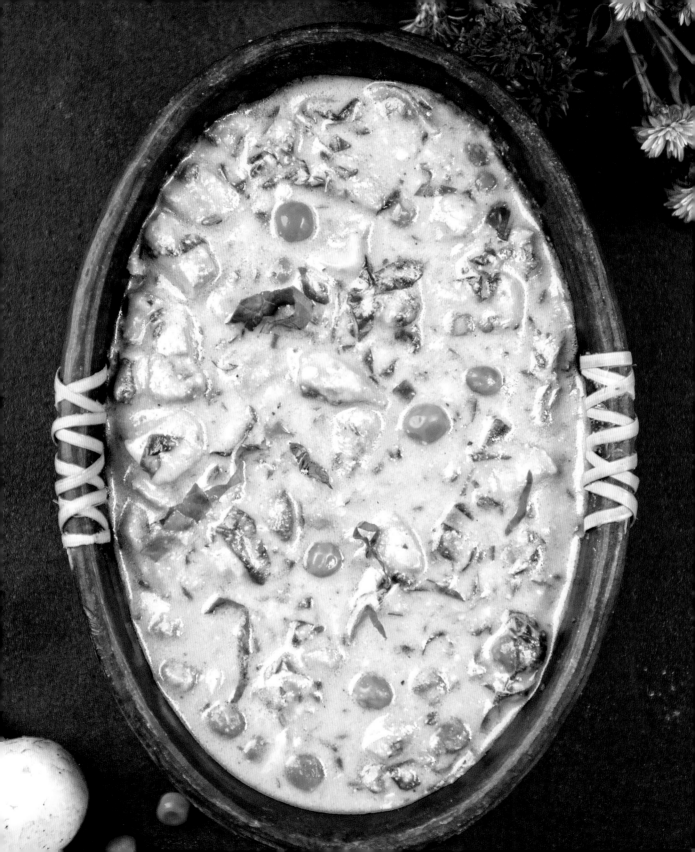

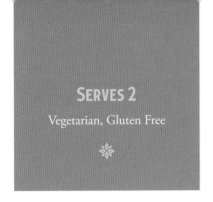

KALE MUSHROOM MATAR MALAI

Kale, Mushroom and Peas Curry

The creamy texture of mushrooms combined with green peas and kale together create a rich, luscious curry. This curry recipe is inspired by the popular Indian dish *methi matar malai*—a winter season favorite when the fresh green peas and the fenugreek leaves are in abundance. The word *malai* indicates the creamy texture of the curry and also symbolizes the presence of cream in the gravy.

2 green cardamom pods

¼ cup (35 g) cashews

1 cup (160 g) sliced white onion

1 tbsp (5 g) chopped fresh ginger

1 tbsp (10 g) chopped garlic

1 mild green chile, such as jalapeño, Thai green chile or serrano pepper, chopped

2¼ tsp (13 g) salt, divided

1 cup (240 ml) water, divided

4 tbsp (55 g) ghee

1 tsp cumin seeds

2 cups (140 g) diced button mushrooms

½ cup (75 g) green peas, fresh or frozen

1 tsp red chili powder

½ tsp ground coriander

1½ cups (100 g) chopped kale

¼ cup (60 ml) light cream (see note)

1 tsp garam masala

In the inner pot of the Instant Pot, combine the green cardamom pods, cashews, onion, ginger, garlic, green chile, ¼ teaspoon of the salt and ¼ cup (60 ml) of the water, and stir. Close the lid. Set the steam valve to the sealing position. Pressure cook at high pressure for 2 minutes. Wait for the natural release of steam.

Transfer to a blender and blend the mixture to a smooth paste.

Set the SAUTÉ mode of the Instant Pot for 5 minutes. Add the ghee to the inner pot. Once the ghee is hot, add the cumin seeds and prepared curry paste. Sauté for 1 minute.

Add the mushrooms and green peas, and sauté for 2 to 3 minutes. Add the remaining ¾ cup (180 ml) of water, remaining 2 teaspoons (12 g) of salt, red chili powder and coriander, and stir to combine.

Close the lid. Set the steam valve to the sealing position. Pressure cook at high pressure for 5 minutes. Let the steam release naturally.

Add the kale, cream and garam masala, and simmer in SAUTÉ mode for 5 minutes.

Serve with naan.

NOTE:

❈ I do not recommend pressure cooking the cream. Usually the dairy ingredients, such as milk or cream, curdle or split while pressure cooking, resulting in tiny bits of cream swimming in the curry.

MIX VEG MASALA

Seasonal Mixed Vegetables Curry

In India, a variety of vegetables are available in abundance throughout the year. This vegetarian curry is a medley of vegetables. There are usually two versions of mixed veg masala—one is a stir-fry and the second one has a gravy. I am sharing with you a curry-licious version of mixed veg masala that is ready in an Instant Pot in under 20 minutes.

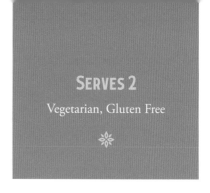

SERVES 2

Vegetarian, Gluten Free

Set the SAUTÉ mode of the Instant Pot for 10 minutes.

Add the oil to the inner pot. Once the oil is hot, add the cumin seeds, nigella seeds and bay leaf, and fry for 10 to 20 seconds.

Add the chopped onion. Sauté for 3 minutes, or until it is lightly browned.

Add the ginger and garlic paste, canned tomato, salt, turmeric, red chili powder and coriander, and sauté for 2 to 3 minutes.

Next, add the quartered onion, baby corn, bell pepper and paneer, and stir to combine.

Add the water and mix. Close the lid. Set the steam valve to the sealing position. Pressure cook at high pressure for 5 minutes. Let the steam release naturally.

Add the diced tomato, cream, ginger, fenugreek leaves and cilantro.

Simmer in SAUTÉ mode for 2 to 3 minutes. Remove and discard the bay leaf before serving.

Serve with any Indian flatbread.

4 tbsp (60 ml) vegetable oil

1 tsp cumin seeds

1 tsp nigella seeds

1 bay leaf

½ cup (80 g) finely chopped yellow onion

1 tbsp (20 g) ginger and garlic paste

½ cup (90 g) canned tomato

1¼ tsp (7 g) salt

1 tsp ground turmeric

½ tsp red chili powder

1 tsp ground coriander

½ cup (80 g) quartered onion

½ cup (84 g) baby corn, cut into ½" (1.3-cm)-long pieces

½ cup (75 g) diced green bell pepper

½ cup (100 g) cubed paneer

½ cup (120 ml) water

½ cup (90 g) seeded and diced tomato

2 tbsp (30 ml) light cream

1 tbsp (5 g) julienned fresh ginger

1 tsp dried fenugreek leaves (kasuri methi)

1 tbsp (1 g) finely chopped fresh cilantro

Kale Boondi Kadhi

Yogurt Curry with Kale

Kadhi is a widely popular Indian stew made with gram (chickpea) flour, dahi (curd) and spices, with crispy *pakora* (fritters) dunked into it. There are many versions of kadhi around the Indian subcontinent. This Instant Pot–friendly kadhi recipe comes with a twist of *boondi*—crispy, tiny, fried balls of gram flour commonly available at Indian grocery stores. The sourness of the dahi, the thickness of the gram flour, the bitterness of the kale, and the spiciness of the boondi balls make this curry delectably savory.

2 cups (480 ml) dahi (curd) or plain Greek yogurt

¼ cup (30 g) gram (chickpea) flour

1 tsp red chili powder

1¼ tsp (7 g) salt, divided

1 cup (240 ml) water, divided

4 tbsp (55 g) ghee

1 tsp ground turmeric

1 tsp black mustard seeds

1 tsp cumin seeds

¼ tsp asafetida

1 tbsp (5 g) grated fresh ginger

2 dried red chiles, such as Kashmiri

1 cup (67 g) chopped kale

½ cup (80 g) boondi balls

In a medium-sized bowl, combine the dahi, gram flour, red chili powder and ¼ teaspoon of the salt. Add ½ cup (120 ml) of the water. Whisk the mixture, using a wire whisk or electric hand mixer, to form a smooth, lump-free batter. Set aside.

Set the SAUTÉ mode of the Instant Pot for 10 minutes.

Add the ghee to the inner pot. Once the ghee is hot, add the turmeric, mustard seeds, cumin seeds, asafetida, ginger and red chiles, and fry for 20 to 30 seconds.

Add the kale and sauté for 1 minute.

Next, slowly with one hand, add the whisked dahl mixture, while with the other hand, using a ladle, stir the curry constantly to prevent the formation of lumps.

Add the remaining ½ cup (120 ml) of water, remaining 1 teaspoon (6 g) of salt and the boondi balls. Let the kadhi simmer until the timer beeps, stirring at regular intervals.

Close the lid. Set the steam valve to the sealing position. Cook in SOUP mode for 5 minutes. Wait for the steam to release naturally.

Serve warm with basmati rice for a simple Indian meal.

SERVES 2

Vegan, Gluten Free

✤

BHAGARA BAINGAN

Sweet and Spicy Baby Eggplant Curry

Apart from *biryani*, Hyderabadi cuisine is also known for its vegetarian delicacies. *Bhagara baingan* is panfried baby *brinjal* (eggplant) cooked in a sweet, spicy coconut and peanut gravy. The curry is often served as a side dish with biryani but tastes even more delicious with basmati rice or Indian flatbread.

4 baby brinjal (eggplants)

4 tbsp (60 ml) vegetable oil

1 cup (160 g) chopped red onion

2 cloves garlic

2 dried red chiles, such as Kashmiri

1 tbsp (5 g) coriander seeds

1 tbsp (8 g) white sesame seeds

2 tbsp (18 g) peanuts, skinned

1 tsp white poppy seeds

1 tsp cumin seeds

¼ tsp fenugreek seeds

2 tbsp (11 g) grated coconut

1 cup (240 ml) water, divided

1¼ tsp (7 g) salt

1 tsp red chili powder

1 tsp ground turmeric

1 tbsp (15 g) tamarind paste

1 tsp light brown sugar or jaggery powder

2 tbsp (2 g) chopped fresh cilantro, for garnish

Wash and pat dry the baby brinjal. Cut an X into the bottom of each brinjal using a knife.

Set the SAUTÉ mode of the Instant Pot for 15 minutes. Add the oil to the inner pot. Once the oil is hot, add the brinjal. Cook on both sides by turning them halfway through; the total cooking time should be 5 to 6 minutes. Transfer the brinjal to a plate and set aside.

Combine the red onion, garlic, red chiles, coriander seeds, sesame seeds, peanuts, poppy seeds, cumin seeds and fenugreek seeds in the inner pot. Sauté until the timer beeps. Add the coconut, and quickly stir the mixture. Do not fry the coconut for too long along with the spices as it could burn quickly; a quick roasting of a few seconds is enough to release the coconut flavor.

Transfer the onion mixture to a blender and blend it into a smooth paste using ¼ cup (60 ml) of the water.

Transfer the paste back to the inner pot. Add the salt, red chili powder, turmeric, tamarind paste, brown sugar and the remaining ¾ cup (180 ml) of the water. Stir to combine.

Arrange the fried brinjal over the curry masala paste. Close the lid. Set the steam valve to the sealing position. Pressure cook at high pressure for 2 minutes. Wait for the natural release of the steam.

Garnish with cilantro. Serve with chapati or paratha.

METHI CHAMAN

Green Paneer Curry

Methi is the Hindi term for fenugreek leaves, and paneer is called *chaman* in Kashmiri. *Methi chaman* is a delicious paneer curry from the Kashmir region. I am sharing a comforting Punjabi version of the curry, cooked with minimal ingredients and full of natural flavors.

SERVES 2

Vegetarian, Gluten Free

❋

Set the SAUTÉ mode of the Instant Pot for 10 minutes.

Add 2 tablespoons (28 g) of the ghee to the inner pot. Once the ghee is hot, add the ginger, garlic, chiles and onion. Sauté for 3 to 4 minutes, or until the onion is lightly browned.

Add the tomato and salt, and cook for 2 minutes, or until the tomato turns soft.

Add the spinach and fenugreek leaves. Stir to combine in the masala.

Add the water and stir. Close the lid. Set the steam valve to the sealing position. Pressure cook at high pressure for 2 minutes. Use a quick manual pressure release.

Transfer the pressure-cooked mixture to a blender. Blend into a smooth paste.

Set the SAUTÉ mode for 5 minutes. Add the remaining 2 tablespoons (27 g) of ghee. Once the ghee is hot, add the bay leaf, cumin seeds, asafetida, blended curry masala paste, red chili powder, cream and garam masala. Stir to combine.

Add the paneer cubes and mix with the curry paste. Let the curry simmer until the timer beeps. Remove and discard the bay leaf before serving.

Serve warm with naan.

NOTE:

❋ For a vegan version of this curry, replace the ghee with vegetable oil, the light cream with thick coconut or almond milk and the paneer with tofu.

4 tbsp (55 g) ghee, divided (see note)

1 tbsp (5 g) chopped fresh ginger

1 tbsp (10 g) chopped garlic

2 mild green chiles, such as jalapeños, Thai green chiles or serrano peppers, chopped

½ cup (80 g) chopped yellow onion

¼ cup (45 g) chopped tomato

1 tsp salt

2 cups (60 g) spinach, chopped

1 cup (55 g) chopped fresh fenugreek leaves

1 cup (240 ml) water

1 bay leaf

1 tsp cumin seeds

¼ tsp asafetida

½ tsp red chili powder

1 tbsp (15 ml) light cream (see note)

1 tsp garam masala

2 cups (400 g) cubed paneer (see note)

DAHI BHINDI

Crispy Okra in a Yogurt Sauce

In the Indian subcontinent, okra (a.k.a. lady's finger) is one of the most cherished vegetables. It is the key ingredient of hundreds of Indian recipes. My favorite is crispy okra cooked in a subtle yogurt sauce, known as *dahi bhindi*. *Dahi* is the local term for "curd"; and *bhindi*, for "okra." Light and refreshing, this vegetarian curry is perfect for a summer lunch.

9 oz (250 g) okra

½ cup (120 ml) dahi (curd) or plain Greek yogurt

1 tbsp (8 g) gram (chickpea) flour

4 tbsp (60 ml) vegetable oil, divided

¼ tsp asafetida

1 tsp cumin seeds

⅓ cup (53 g) diced yellow onion

1 tsp ginger and garlic paste

2 mild green chiles, such as jalapeños, Thai green chiles or serrano peppers, sliced

1 tsp ground turmeric

1 tsp red chili powder

1 tsp ground coriander

1 tsp salt

¼ cup (60 ml) water

1 tsp garam masala

1 tsp dried fenugreek leaves (kasuri methi)

2 tbsp (2 g) chopped fresh cilantro

Rinse the okra with water, then dry it with a clean kitchen towel.

Make sure that there is no moisture or water droplets on the okra before you start to chop it. Trim off the head and tail of the okra. Chop the okra into 1-inch (2.5-cm)-long pieces. Set aside.

In a small bowl, whisk together the dahi and gram flour to make a smooth, lump-free paste. Set aside.

Set the SAUTÉ mode of the Instant Pot for 10 minutes. Add 2 tablespoons (30 ml) of the oil to the inner pot. Once the oil is hot, add the okra and fry, turning at regular intervals, until it changes color and is cooked and softened, about 5 minutes. Transfer to a plate and set aside.

Add the remaining 2 tablespoons (30 ml) of oil to the inner pot along with asafetida, cumin seeds and onion. Sauté for 3 minutes, or until the onion becomes translucent and tender.

Add the ginger and garlic paste and green chiles and fry for 1 minute.

Next, add the curd mixture, turmeric, red chili powder, coriander and salt, while stirring the curry constantly.

Add the water and stir to combine. Close the lid. Set the steam valve to the sealing position. Cook in SOUP mode for 5 minutes. Release the steam manually.

Add the fried okra, garam masala, fenugreek leaves and cilantro. Mix nicely.

Serve with chapati for a hearty meal.

CHICKEN FROM MY KITCHEN

In India, chicken is one of the oldest domesticated birds. There are tons and tons of Indian curry recipes with chicken as the key ingredient, which you can make effortlessly in an Instant Pot. In this chapter, I am sharing a collection of unique chicken curry recipes that you will not find in a restaurant or takeaway joint. A lot of these were developed during the Mughal era. And later, the European influence also defined many chicken curry recipes, which are now part of modern Indian cuisine.

In this chapter, chicken curry recipes depict the diverse cooking styles in India; for instance, Delhi-style Murgh Shah Jahani (page 103) with Mughali fineness, heavy-on-whole-spices Chicken Chettinad Masala (page 107) from Tamil Nadu's most affluent Chettiar trading community, or Kashmiri Chicken Rista (page 111)—a unique chicken meatball curry cooked with minimal spices. Each of these chicken recipes is distinctive in terms of taste, texture and ingredients and has an exciting tale to tell.

Chicken is one of the most popular nonvegetarian ingredients (you can guess that from the popularity of our butter chicken). There are many reasons for the popularity of chicken in India—first, the mild taste of poultry blends perfectly with bold Indian curries. Second, it is readily available and inexpensive, and the white meat is suitable even for the hot and humid summer season. Third, and the most crucial reason, is that chicken does not fall under any religious food taboos, unlike the holy cow or pork. Hence, despite their religious differences, all the meat-eaters in India find harmony when it comes to chicken—so it deserves a dedicated chapter in my cookbook to showcase the variety of ways in which you can make a delicious chicken curry.

MURGH SHAH JAHANI

Mughlai-Style Chicken Curry

The reign of Mughal emperor Shah Jahan is well known for the Taj Mahal, and the gastronomic pinnacle of Mughlai cuisine. Many chicken curries, kormas, biryani, kebabs and desserts were developed in his royal kitchen, and to date, are popular across India as the symbol of Mughal cuisine. *Murgh Shah Jahani* is one such royal delicacy from his kitchen. It is a rich, subtle, aromatic, mildly spicy curry. One bite and you will be transported to the royal gala feast of Mughal emperors. This chicken curry lives up to its name.

4 tbsp (55 g) ghee

1 tsp white poppy seeds

1 tsp black peppercorns

1 (1" [2.5-cm])-long piece cinnamon stick

2 tsp (4 g) cumin seeds

2 tsp (4 g) coriander seeds

10 green cardamom pods

2 tbsp (30 ml) dahi (curd) or plain Greek yogurt

9 oz (250 g) skinless, bone-in chicken, cut into 1¼" to 1½" (3- to 4-cm) bone-in pieces (see note)

2 tsp (12 g) salt, divided

1 cup (160 g) sliced yellow onion

1 tbsp (5 g) chopped fresh ginger

1 tbsp (10 g) chopped garlic

1 cup (240 ml) water, divided

¼ tsp saffron strands

1 tbsp (15 ml) warm water

½ tsp red chili powder

¼ tsp rose water or kewra essence

1 tbsp (7 g) almond slivers, for garnish

Set the SAUTÉ mode of the Instant Pot for 10 minutes.

Add the ghee to the inner pot. Once the ghee is hot, add the poppy seeds, peppercorns, cinnamon stick, cumin seeds, coriander seeds and cardamom pods. Sauté for 2 minutes. Transfer the roasted spices to a blender along with the dahi. Blend into a smooth paste.

In a medium-sized bowl, marinate the chicken with the spice paste and 1 teaspoon of the salt; cover and chill in the refrigerator for at least 1 hour.

To the same inner pot as used for the spice paste, add the onion and fry until golden, 6 to 8 minutes. Add the ginger and garlic, and sauté for 30 to 40 seconds.

Transfer the fried onion mixture to a blender. Make a smooth paste, using 1 to 2 tablespoons (15 to 30 ml) of the water.

Soak the saffron in 1 tablespoon (15 ml) of warm water. Set aside.

Set the SAUTÉ mode for 8 minutes.

Add the marinated chicken to the empty inner pot. Sear the chicken for 3 to 4 minutes, or until the juices are released and the chicken becomes almost opaque. Add the fried onion paste, remaining teaspoon of salt, red chili powder and ½ cup (120 ml) of the water, and mix.

Close the lid. Set the steam valve to the sealing position. Set to pressure cook on high pressure for 2 minutes. Cook the chicken until the timer beeps. Wait for the natural release of steam.

Add the soaked saffron with its liquid and the rose water, and stir to combine. If you want to make extra gravy, add the remaining water at this stage.

Let the curry simmer in SAUTÉ mode for 5 minutes. Garnish with the almond slivers.

NOTE:

✤ Curry-cut chicken (skinless, bone-in chicken thigh or leg) is perfect for this curry. Avoid using lean chicken breast or boneless pieces.

Sunday Chicken Curry

Indian Masala Chicken Curry

During the '90s, with economic development, there was an upsurge in nuclear, middle-class families. With Sunday being the only work and school holiday, a tradition of comforting Sunday meals that one could share with the family started, and eventually it became a weekly ritual for many families, including mine. This is my family's favorite Sunday afternoon lunch with steamed basmati rice. If you are looking for an Instant Pot–friendly Indian chicken curry for everyday cooking, then this recipe is worth bookmarking.

SERVES 2

Gluten Free

In a blender or food processor, make a paste of the chopped tomato, red chiles, garlic and ginger, using 4 tablespoons (60 ml) of the water. Set aside.

Set the SAUTÉ mode of the Instant Pot for 15 minutes.

Add the oil to the inner pot. Once the oil is smoking hot, add the red onion. Fry the red onion until golden, 6 to 8 minutes. Once fried, transfer to a blender. Blend into a smooth paste, using 1 to 2 tablespoons (15 to 30 ml) of water.

Meanwhile, in the empty inner pot, combine the bay leaf, cinnamon stick, the tomato-chile paste you previously made, red chili powder, turmeric and coriander. Fry for 2 to 3 minutes.

Add the chicken pieces and salt. Sear the chicken while sautéing until the juices are released and the chicken becomes almost opaque, about 5 minutes. Do not add any water.

Next, add the blended onion paste, and then ¼ cup (60 ml) of the water. Mix nicely.

Close the lid. Set the steam valve to the sealing position. Pressure cook at high pressure for 2 minutes. Wait for the natural release of steam.

Add the garam masala, fenugreek leaves and green chiles, and mix.

Let the curry simmer in SAUTÉ mode for 5 minutes. At this stage, if you need extra gravy, add up to ¼ cup (60 ml) of the remaining water and simmer the curry. Remove and discard the bay leaf before serving.

Garnish with the cilantro. Serve with rice.

1 cup (180 g) chopped tomato

2 dried Kashmiri red chiles

4 cloves garlic

1 tbsp (5 g) chopped fresh ginger

½ cup (120 ml) water, divided, plus 5 to 6 tbsp (75 to 90 ml), divided, for blending

¼ cup (60 ml) mustard oil

1 cup (160 g) sliced red onion

1 bay leaf

1 (1" [2.5-cm])-long piece cinnamon stick

1 tsp Kashmiri red chili powder

1 tsp ground turmeric

1 tsp ground coriander

9 oz (250 g) bone-in chicken, cut into 1¼" to 1½" (3- to 4-cm) bone-in pieces

2 tsp (12 g) salt

1 tsp garam masala

1 tbsp (1 g) dried fenugreek leaves (kasuri methi)

2 mild green chiles, such as jalapeños, Thai green chiles or serrano peppers, sliced

1 tbsp (1 g) chopped fresh cilantro, for garnish

Chicken Chettinad Masala

South India–Style Spicy Chicken Curry

Chicken Chettinad masala is a traditional chicken curry from the region of Chettinad in Tamil Nadu. During the ancient days, the Chettiar community were the affluent traders of spices, and the moneylenders. Today, the Chettinad region is known for its rich cultural heritage and food. This dish is the flag bearer of Chettiar-style cooking. It clearly defines the difference between the taste and cooking of northern and southern India. If you are new to the world of spicy curries, I suggest reducing the amount of chiles and pepper in the recipe according to your taste preference.

1 tsp fennel seeds

1 tsp cumin seeds

1 tsp coriander seeds

2 tsp (3 g) black peppercorns

4 dried red chiles

4 cloves garlic

1 tbsp (5 g) chopped fresh ginger

½ cup (120 ml) water, plus 1 to 2 tbsp (15 to 30 ml) for blending

4 tbsp (60 ml) mustard oil or (55 g) coconut oil

1 (1" [2.5-cm])-long piece cinnamon stick

2 green cardamom pods

5 to 6 curry leaves

1 cup (160 g) finely chopped red onion

½ cup (90 g) chopped fresh tomato, blended to a paste

1¼ tsp (7 g) salt

½ tsp ground turmeric

9 oz (250 g) bone-in chicken, cut into 1¼" to 1½" (3- to 4-cm) bone-in pieces

Set the SAUTÉ mode of the Instant Pot for 15 minutes.

In the inner pot, combine the fennel, cumin and coriander seeds, peppercorns, red chiles, garlic and ginger. Dry roast for 1 minute to release the aroma.

Transfer to a blender. Blend into a coarse paste, using 1 to 2 tablespoons (15 to 30 ml) of water. Transfer to a small bowl and set aside.

Meanwhile, add the oil to the empty inner pot. Once the oil is hot, add the cinnamon stick, cardamom pods, curry leaves and red onion. Fry the onion for 4 to 5 minutes, or until it browns. Add the blended tomato, salt and turmeric, and sauté for 2 to 3 minutes.

Next, add the chicken. Sear the chicken pieces by sautéing until they become almost opaque and start to release liquid, 3 to 4 minutes.

Add the blended masala paste and ½ cup (120 ml) of water to the chicken mixture. Stir to combine.

Close the lid. Set the steam valve to the sealing position. Pressure cook at high pressure for 2 minutes. Wait for the natural release of the steam.

Simmer the curry in SAUTÉ mode for 2 minutes.

Serve with rice or dosa.

NOTE:

✻ You can add ¼ cup (120 ml) of coconut milk to flavor the curry and balance the heat of the spices.

GREEN CHICKEN CURRY

Chicken in a Green Curry Sauce

The refreshing taste of mint combined with the subtle heat of green chiles and the creaminess of coconut milk create a delectable green (*hariyali*) chicken curry. Full of fresh flavors, this dish is perfect for a summer lunch or a quick weeknight dinner; it is ready in an Instant Pot in less than 30 minutes. My only tip: Do not cook the curry for too long, as the green herb paste will start to turn black or gray.

SERVES 2

Gluten Free

In a blender, make a smooth paste of the cilantro, mint, chiles, ginger and garlic, using 4 tablespoons (60 ml) of water. Do not blend for too long, as heat turns green herbs black and bitter.

Set the SAUTÉ mode of the Instant Pot for 10 minutes.

Add the oil to the inner pot. Once the oil is hot, add the onion and fry for 4 to 5 minutes, or until lightly golden.

Next, add the chicken. Sear the chicken pieces by sautéing for 3 to 4 minutes, or until they become almost opaque and start to release liquid.

Add the blended green curry paste, salt, red chili powder and the ½ cup (120 ml) of water. Stir to combine.

Close the lid. Set the steam valve to the sealing position. Pressure cook at high pressure for 4 minutes. Wait for the natural release of the steam.

Add the coconut cream and black pepper, and stir to combine.

Simmer the curry in SAUTÉ mode for 4 to 5 minutes.

Serve with rice.

1 cup (16 g) fresh cilantro leaves

¼ cup (10 g) fresh mint leaves

2 mild green chiles, such as jalapeños, Thai green chiles or serrano peppers, chopped

1 tbsp (5 g) chopped fresh ginger

1 tbsp (10 g) chopped garlic

½ cup (120 ml) water, plus 4 tbsp (60 ml) for blending

4 tbsp (55 g) coconut oil

1 cup (160 g) chopped yellow onion

9 oz (250 g) boneless chicken, cut into 1" to 1¼" (2.5- to 3-cm) pieces

1 tsp salt

¼ tsp red chili powder

¼ cup (60 ml) coconut cream

1½ tsp (3 g) freshly ground black pepper

CHICKEN RISTA

Chicken Meatballs in Red Sauce

Chicken rista is a Kashmiri-style meatball curry often served as part of the Kashmiri *waazwan*, a several-course royal feast prepared by special chefs known as *waaza*. Unlike other meatball curries, here the chicken meatballs are poached in the curry itself, neither fried nor cooked separately.

2 black cardamom pods, divided

4 green cardamom pods

9 oz (250 g) ground chicken (see note)

2 tsp (2 g) ground ginger, divided

2 tsp (12 g) salt, divided

½ tsp garam masala

¼ cup (55 g) unsalted butter or margarine

4 cups (960 ml) water, divided, plus 4 tbsp (60 ml) for blending

¼ tsp saffron strands

1 tbsp (15 ml) warm water

4 tbsp (55 g) ghee

1 cup (160 g) chopped yellow onion

1 tbsp (5 g) chopped fresh ginger

1 tbsp (10 g) chopped garlic

1 tsp cumin seeds

1 (1" [2.5-cm])-long piece cinnamon stick

4 whole cloves

1 tbsp (8 g) Kashmiri red chili powder, divided

1 tsp ground fennel

2 tbsp (2 g) chopped fresh cilantro

In a spice grinder, make a powder of one of the black cardamom pods and all four green cardamom pods.

In a medium-sized bowl, combine the ground chicken, freshly ground cardamom powder, 1 teaspoon of the ground ginger, 1 teaspoon of the salt and the garam masala. Mix nicely.

Next, add the butter to the ground chicken, using a meat pounder to mix it evenly into the chicken. Form 1 tablespoon (15 g) of ground chicken into a ½-inch (1.25-cm) meatball. Repeat to form the other meatballs; you should end up with 10 to 12.

Pour 2 cups (480 ml) of water into a wide bowl. Place the meatballs in the water. Set aside.

Soak the saffron in the 1 tablespoon (15 ml) of warm water. Set aside.

Set the SAUTÉ mode of the Instant Pot for 20 minutes.

Add the ghee to the inner pot. Once hot, add the onion and fry for 4 to 5 minutes, or until golden.

Add the fresh ginger and garlic, and fry for 1 minute. Transfer to a blender (reserving the ghee inside the inner pot of the Instant Pot) and blend it to a paste using 4 tablespoons (60 ml) of water.

Meanwhile, to the remaining ghee in the inner pot, add the cumin seeds, cinnamon stick, remaining black cardamom pod, cloves and 1½ teaspoons (4 g) of the red chili powder. Sauté for 30 to 40 seconds.

Add the onion paste, 2 cups (480 ml) of water, remaining 1½ teaspoons (4 g) of red chile powder, fennel, remaining teaspoon of salt and remaining teaspoon of ground ginger.

Stir and allow the curry to simmer. Once the curry thickens a bit, gently drop the meatballs into the curry. Allow them to simmer in the curry. This process will poach the meatballs and cook them. Cover the Instant Pot with a glass lid while the meatballs are simmering. They do not take more than 5 to 6 minutes to be fully cooked. After adding the meatballs to the curry, do not stir it vigorously, as the meatballs might break apart.

Add the soaked saffron with its liquid and the cilantro. Serve with rice.

NOTE:

✳ **I do not recommend using frozen ground chicken for this recipe. Freshly ground meat will give you perfectly moist meatballs.**

CHICKEN KA SALAN

Sweet and Spicy Chicken Curry

Hyderabad was once the largest princely state of the Indian subcontinent and renowned for its food. Hyderabadi cuisine has the influence of Hindu, Arab and Middle Eastern styles of cooking. *Salan* is one of the most popular side dishes served with Hyderabadi biryani. It can be vegetarian or nonvegetarian. Chicken ka salan is a sweet, spicy, delicious curry with the flavor of peanuts, sesame seeds, coconut, chiles, tamarind and many more intriguing ingredients. Trust me, you can make this compliment-worthy delicious dish to perfection in an Instant Pot. All you have to do is follow this recipe to a T.

SERVES 2

Gluten Free

❁

Set the SAUTÉ mode of the Instant Pot for 15 minutes.

Add the coriander, cumin, sesame and fenugreek seeds, peanuts, coconut, ginger and garlic. Dry roast for 1 minute. Transfer to a blender. Make a paste, using 4 tablespoons (60 ml) of water. Set aside until you're ready to use it. Alternatively, you can dry roast the ingredients for the masala paste separately in a skillet over medium heat.

Add the oil to the empty inner pot. Once the oil is hot, add the cloves, cardamom pods, bay leaf and red onion. Fry until the onion is lightly golden, 3 to 4 minutes.

Add the tomato, red chili powder, turmeric, tamarind paste and ¼ teaspoon of the salt.

Fry for 2 to 3 minutes, then add the chicken pieces. Sauté for 2 minutes, or until they become almost opaque and start to release liquid.

Add the remaining teaspoon of salt, 1 cup (240 ml) of the water and the blended masala paste. Stir to mix.

Close the lid. Set the steam valve to the sealing position. Pressure cook at high pressure for 2 minutes. Let the steam release naturally.

Add the green chiles and cilantro, and simmer in SAUTÉ mode for 5 minutes. Remove and discard the bay leaf before serving.

Serve with rice.

1 tbsp (5 g) coriander seeds

1 tbsp (6 g) cumin seeds

3 tbsp (24 g) white sesame seeds

¼ tsp fenugreek seeds

1 tbsp (9 g) peanuts, skinned

1 tbsp grated or desiccated coconut

1 tbsp (5 g) chopped fresh ginger

5 cloves garlic

1 cup (240 ml) water, plus 4 tbsp (60 ml) for blending

¼ cup (55 g) coconut oil

4 whole cloves

4 green cardamom pods

1 black cardamom pod

1 bay leaf

1 cup (160 g) finely chopped red onion

½ cup (122 g) canned crushed tomato

1 tsp red chili powder

1 tsp ground turmeric

1 tbsp (15 g) tamarind paste

1¼ tsp (7 g) salt, divided

9 oz (250 g) bone-in chicken, cut into 1¼" to 1½" (3- to 4-cm) bone-in pieces

2 mild to medium-hot green chiles, such as jalapeños, Thai green chiles or serrano peppers, sliced

1 tbsp (1 g) chopped fresh cilantro

MURGH CHOLAY CURRY

Chicken Curry with Chickpeas

This is a Punjabi-style chicken and chickpeas curry. At first, the combination may sound odd, but it is deliciously savory. The dish comes from the Punjab region of Pakistan. Nowadays, very few Punjabi families make this special curry, but it is one of my favorite Instant Pot chicken curries. The chickpeas and chicken are cooked to perfection in the Instant Pot, giving the dish a perfect texture. Whenever I make it, the time of India's partition and its aftermath's effect on the lives of people is our dinner table conversation.

9 oz (250 g) bone-in chicken, cut into 1¼" to 1½" (3- to 4-cm) bone-in pieces (see note)

1½ tsp (4 g) red chili powder, divided

1 tsp garam masala, divided

2 tbsp (40 g) ginger and garlic paste, divided

4 tbsp (55 g) ghee

4 whole cloves

1 bay leaf

1 tsp cumin seeds

1 cup (160 g) chopped red onion

½ cup (90 g) canned tomato

1½ tsp (2 g) ground turmeric

1 tsp ground coriander

1¼ tsp (7 g) salt, divided

1 cup (240 g) canned chickpeas

1 cup (240 ml) water

2 mild to medium-hot green chiles, such as jalapeños, Thai green chiles or serrano peppers, sliced

1 tbsp (1 g) dried fenugreek leaves (kasuri methi)

2 tbsp (2 g) chopped fresh cilantro

In a medium-sized bowl, marinate the chicken pieces with ½ teaspoon of the red chili powder, ½ teaspoon of the garam masala and 1 tablespoon (20 g) of the ginger and garlic paste. Cover and chill in the refrigerator for 1 to 2 hours.

Set the SAUTÉ mode of the Instant Pot for 15 minutes.

Add the ghee to the inner pot. Once the ghee is hot, add the cloves, bay leaf, cumin seeds and red onion. Fry until the onion is lightly golden.

Add the remaining tablespoon (20 g) of ginger and garlic paste, tomato, remaining teaspoon of red chili powder, turmeric, coriander and ¼ teaspoon of the salt. Fry for 2 minutes.

Add the marinated chicken pieces. Sauté for 3 to 4 minutes, or until they become almost opaque and start to release liquid.

Drain all the liquid from the canned chickpeas. Rinse them with water. Add the chickpeas to the inner pot. Add the water. Stir to mix.

Close the lid. Set the steam valve to the sealing position. Pressure cook at high pressure for 2 minutes. Wait for the natural release of the steam.

Set the SAUTÉ mode for 4 minutes. Add the remaining ½ teaspoon of garam masala, remaining teaspoon of salt or to taste, green chiles, fenugreek leaves and cilantro. Simmer the curry until the timer beeps. Remove and discard the bay leaf before serving.

Serve with naan or rice.

NOTE:

✻ Chicken leg pieces, drumsticks or thighs work best for this curry recipe.

MALABAR CHICKEN CURRY

Chicken Curry in a Creamy Coconut Curry Paste

From the time of the East India Company, the Malabar district has been of utmost historic importance and well known for its iconic traveler's paradise—the Western Ghats. Seafood and coconut are the two ingredients found in abundance along the Malabar coast. This is a typical coastal-style chicken curry flavored with a special ground paste and coconut milk that you can make with ease in an Instant Pot without spending hours in the kitchen.

SERVES 2

Gluten Free

✳

Set the sauté mode of the Instant Pot for 8 minutes.

In the inner pot, combine the coconut, coriander seeds, black peppercorns, cinnamon stick and red chiles. Fry for 40 to 50 seconds to release the aroma of the spices. Transfer to a blender.

Add 4 tablespoons (55 g) of the coconut oil to the empty inner pot. Add ½ cup (80 g) of the onion and fry until lightly golden. Add the ginger and sauté until the timer beeps.

Transfer the fried onion mixture to the same blender as the spices. Blend into a smooth paste, using 2 to 4 tablespoons (30 to 60 ml) of water. Set aside.

Set the sauté mode for 10 minutes. Heat the remaining 2 tablespoons (38 g) of oil.

Add the mustard seeds, curry leaves and remaining ½ cup (80 g) of onion. Fry until the onion becomes translucent. Add the tomato, turmeric, red chili powder and salt. Sauté for 2 to 3 minutes, or until the tomato is completely mashed up.

Add the chicken. Sauté the pieces for 3 to 4 minutes, or until they become almost opaque. Add the onion and spice mixture as well as the ¼ cup (60 ml) of water, and stir to mix. Close the lid. Set the steam valve to the sealing position. Pressure cook at high pressure for 2 minutes. Wait for the natural release of steam.

Add the coconut milk. Simmer the curry in sauté mode for 5 minutes.

Serve with dosa, *appam* or *parotta*.

¼ cup (21 g) grated coconut

4 tsp (7 g) coriander seeds

1 tsp black peppercorns

1 (1" [2.5-cm])-long piece cinnamon stick

2 dried red chiles

6 tbsp (83 g) coconut oil, divided

1 cup (160 g) finely chopped yellow onion, divided

1 tbsp (5 g) chopped fresh ginger

¼ cup (60 ml) water, plus 2 to 4 tbsp (30 to 60 ml) for blending

1 tsp black mustard seeds

6 curry leaves

½ cup (90 g) chopped tomato

1 tsp ground turmeric

1 tsp red chili powder

1¼ tsp (7 g) salt

9 oz (250 g) bone-in chicken, cut into 1¼" to 1½" (3- to 4-cm) bone-in pieces

¼ cup (60 ml) coconut milk

Chicken Kali Mirch

Creamy Black Pepper Sauce Chicken

This chicken curry revolves around pepper—the spice that brought Europeans to the Indian shore. After butter chicken, I must say, kali mirch chicken is second on the popularity charts of chicken curries. This creamy, pepper-spiced dish is perfect for those who are looking for an Indian chicken curry with minimal spices. Serve it with a fragrant pilaf or basmati rice for a delicious Indian curry night meal.

6 tbsp (83 g) ghee, divided

9 oz (250 g) bone-in chicken, cut into 1¼" to 1½" (3- to 4-cm) bone-in pieces

1 tsp caraway seeds

4 green cardamom pods

2 cups (320 g) minced white onion

1 tbsp (5 g) minced fresh ginger

1 tbsp (6 g) freshly ground black pepper

1 tsp salt

¼ cup (60 ml) water

1 cup (240 ml) dahi (curd) or plain Greek yogurt

½ tsp garam masala

2 mild green chiles, such as jalapeños, Thai green chiles or serrano peppers, sliced

1 tbsp (1 g) dried fenugreek leaves (kasuri methi)

2 tbsp (30 ml) light cream

Set the SAUTÉ mode of the Instant Pot for 15 minutes.

Add 2 tablespoons (28 g) of the ghee to the inner pot. Once the ghee is hot, add the chicken pieces. Sauté for 3 to 4 minutes, or until they become almost opaque. Transfer to a plate. Set aside.

Add the remaining 4 tbsp (55 g) of ghee to the pot. Add the caraway seeds and cardamom pods, and sauté for 20 to 30 seconds. Add the onion and fry until lightly golden. Add the ginger. Fry for 30 seconds. Next, add the chicken back to the pot along with the black pepper, salt and water, and stir to mix.

Close the lid. Set the steam valve to the sealing position. Pressure cook at high pressure for 4 minutes. Wait for the natural release of steam.

Whisk the dahi until smooth and lump free. Add it slowly to the chicken mixture along with the garam masala, green chiles and fenugreek leaves. Let the curry simmer in SAUTÉ mode for 8 minutes. Finally, add the cream and give it a good mix.

Serve with naan or your flatbread of choice.

ACHARI CHICKEN

Indian Pickle Spiced Chicken Curry

Indian pickles are called *achar* in Hindi. The word *achari* describes the pickle-like taste or aroma of a dish. After one bite, this tantalizing dish will remind you of Indian pickles. The smoky flavor; such spices as nigella seeds (*kalonji*), fenugreek seeds and fennel seeds; and an easy Instant Pot–friendly cooking process are the highlights of this unique chicken curry.

SERVES 2

Gluten Free

❈

Set the SAUTÉ mode of the Instant Pot for 15 minutes.

Add the oil to the inner pot. Once the oil is hot, add the mustard, nigella, cumin, fennel and fenugreek seeds, and the dried red chiles. Sauté for 40 to 50 seconds.

Add the red onion and fry until golden.

Next, add the ginger and garlic paste. Sauté for 40 to 50 seconds.

Add the tomato, turmeric, red chili powder, coriander and salt. Sauté for 2 minutes, or until the masala comes together and the raw smell wafts away.

Add the chicken pieces. Sauté until the timer beeps. Add the water and mix. Close the lid. Set the steam valve to the sealing position. Pressure cook at high pressure for 2 minutes. Wait for the natural release of steam.

Whisk the dahi nicely. Add it slowly to the curry, stirring constantly to prevent any lump formation, along with the green chiles, ginger and fenugreek leaves. Simmer the curry in SAUTÉ mode for 6 minutes, stirring at regular intervals.

Garnish with the cilantro. Serve with rice.

NOTE:

❈ **Do not pressure cook the dahi as it might curdle, leaving you with an unpleasant curry.**

4 tbsp (60 ml) mustard oil

1 tsp black mustard seeds

1 tsp nigella seeds

1 tsp cumin seeds

1 tsp fennel seeds

¼ tsp fenugreek seeds

4 dried Kashmiri red chiles

1 cup (160 g) finely chopped red onion

1 tbsp (20 g) ginger and garlic paste

1 cup (180 g) canned tomato

1 tsp ground turmeric

1 tsp red chili powder

1 tsp ground coriander

1½ tsp (7 g) salt

9 oz (250 g) chicken pieces, bone-in or boneless

½ cup (120 ml) water

⅓ cup (80 ml) dahi (curd) or plain Greek yogurt (see note)

2 mild green chiles, such as jalapeños, Thai green chiles or serrano peppers, sliced

2 tbsp (10 g) julienned fresh ginger

1 tbsp (1 g) dried fenugreek leaves (kasuri methi)

2 tbsp (2 g) chopped fresh cilantro, for garnish

FOR
MEAT
LOVERS

This chapter will inspire you to try glorious Indian meat curries in an Instant Pot without much hassle, and these recipes are bound to become your favorites for family dinner, curry night or Indian-style dinner parties.

In India, *mutton* is the generic term used for goat meat and lamb, though I know the terminology is not correct. So, don't get confused! Also, in India, beef, pork, lamb and goat meat are not sold under the same roof due to religious food taboos.

When it comes to Indian meat curries, slow cooking is the most delicious route to make a quintessential dish. In my great-grandmother's kitchen, meat curry was always slow-cooked in a heavy metal vessel over the open wood fire. As modernization entered our traditional kitchen, my mother started cooking meat curries in a stovetop pressure cooker. But that requires a lot of experience and often you will end up with overcooked meat.

Instant Pot is my one-stop solution for all the meat curries, especially the Slow Cooker Goat Curry (page 125). Reason: The SLOW COOK mode makes the curry flavors penetrate the meat's fibers, making it juicy, tender and savory without the risk of overcooking. Trust me, when it comes to cooking meat curry in an Instant Pot, a combination of the PRESSURE COOK and SLOW COOK modes will give you gratifying results. In my opinion, an Instant Pot transforms an ordinary meat dish into an exemplary one.

SLOW COOKER GOAT CURRY

Slow-Cooked Masala Goat Curry

When it comes to goat curries, there are tons of unique, traditional recipes from every region of India. This is a slow-cooked curry in simple onion and tomato masala, but there is nothing basic about the flavors of the curry. The SLOW COOK mode of an Instant Pot helps the masala penetrate within the layers of the meat, making it juicy and perfectly tender at the same time.

9 oz (250 g) bone-in goat meat, cut into 2" (5-cm) pieces

⅓ cup (80 ml) dahi (curd) or plain Greek yogurt

1 tsp Kashmiri red chili powder

¼ tsp garam masala

2 tsp (12 g) salt, divided

1 (1" [2.5-cm])-long piece cinnamon stick

4 whole cloves

2 green cardamom pods

1 black cardamom pod

4 tbsp (60 ml) mustard oil

1 bay leaf

1½ cups (240 g) chopped red onion

1 tbsp (20 g) ginger and garlic paste

½ cup (90 g) chopped tomato

1 tsp red chili powder

½ tsp ground turmeric

1 tsp ground coriander

1 cup (240 ml) water

2 mild to medium-hot green chiles, such as jalapeños, Thai green chiles or serrano peppers, sliced

2 tbsp (2 g) chopped fresh cilantro, for garnish

Clean and pat dry the meat pieces. In a medium-sized bowl, combine the dahi, Kashmiri red chili powder, garam masala and 1 teaspoon of the salt, and marinate the meat in this mixture, then cover and chill in the refrigerator for at least 1 hour or best overnight.

In the Instant Pot set to SAUTÉ mode or in a skillet over medium heat, dry roast the cinnamon stick, cloves and cardamom pods for 40 to 50 seconds, stirring them for even roasting and to prevent burning. Then, grind the mixture to a coarse powder, using a spice grinder. Do not add water. Set aside.

Set the SAUTÉ mode of the Instant Pot for 20 minutes. Add the oil to the inner pot. Once the oil is smoking hot, add the bay leaf and red onion. Fry the onion for 5 minutes, or until lightly golden. Add the ginger and garlic paste, and fry for 40 to 50 seconds.

Add the marinated meat and sear on all sides for a total of 5 minutes. The color will change to light brown.

Next, add the tomato, red chili powder, turmeric and coriander, and sauté for 2 to 3 minutes.

Add the water. Close the lid. Set the SLOW COOK mode for 5 hours. When that time is up, check the meat for doneness. It should be fibrous and well done.

Add the spice powder mixture and green chiles, and simmer the curry in SAUTÉ mode for 10 minutes. Remove and discard the bay leaf before serving.

Garnish with the cilantro and serve.

Keema Methi Matar Masala

Ground Goat Curry with Peas and Fenugreek Leaves

In the Indian subcontinent, ground meat is called *keema* or *qeema*. From kebabs to kofta to curry, it is used in a variety of delicious dishes. *Keema methi matar masala* is a flavorful Punjabi-style ground meat curry with fresh fenugreek leaves and green peas. This recipe is a wintertime family favorite with piping hot *phulka* or paratha. You can use any ground red meat for this recipe. The best part of cooking keema curry in an Instant Pot is that the ground meat does not taste bland at all; with each bite, you get a real burst of flavors.

SERVES 2

Gluten Free

In a medium-sized bowl, combine the ground meat with the dahi, 1 teaspoon of the turmeric, 1 teaspoon of the red chili powder, the coriander, 1½ teaspoons (10 g) of the ginger and garlic paste and ¼ teaspoon of the salt and let marinate, covered, in the refrigerator for 1 hour or overnight.

Set the SAUTÉ mode of the Instant Pot for 20 minutes. Add the oil to the inner pot. Once the oil is smoking hot, add the bay leaf, cloves, cardamom pod and red onion. Fry the onion for 3 to 4 minutes, or until lightly golden. Add the remaining tablespoon (20 g) of ginger and garlic paste. Fry for 40 to 50 seconds.

Next, add the tomato, remaining teaspoon of red chili powder, remaining 1 teaspoon of salt and remaining ¼ teaspoon of turmeric, and sauté for 2 to 3 minutes.

Add the marinated ground meat. Sauté the ground meat for 5 minutes, or until it becomes lightly browned. Add the green peas and water, and stir to mix.

Close the lid. Set the steam valve to the sealing position. Pressure cook at high pressure for 8 minutes. Wait for the natural release of steam.

Add the fresh fenugreek leaves, garam masala and green chiles, and mix.

Simmer the curry in SAUTÉ mode for 5 minutes. Remove and discard the bay leaf before serving.

Garnish with the cilantro and serve.

NOTE:

❊ **Alternatively, you can use ground lamb or turkey for this curry recipe.**

9 oz (250 g) ground goat meat (see note)

2 tbsp (30 ml) dahi (curd) or plain Greek yogurt

1¼ tsp (4 g) ground turmeric, divided

2 tsp (5 g) red chili powder, divided

1 tsp ground coriander

1½ tbsp (30 g) ginger and garlic paste, divided

1¼ tsp (7 g) salt, divided

4 tbsp (60 ml) mustard oil

1 bay leaf

2 whole cloves

1 black cardamom pod

1 cup (160 g) finely chopped red onion

¼ cup (45 g) chopped tomato

1 cup (150 g) green peas

⅓ cup (80 ml) water

1 cup (55 g) chopped fresh fenugreek leaves

1 tsp garam masala

2 mild to medium-hot green chiles, such as jalapeños, Thai green chiles, or serrano peppers, chopped

2 tbsp (2 g) chopped fresh cilantro, for garnish

KUNDAN KALIYA

Royal Golden Lamb Curry

Kundan kaliya, which translates to "golden curry," is symbolic of how an ordinary meat curry can be transformed into a royal delicacy. From the ancient Awadhi cuisine of Lucknow to the nawabs of Bengal, all patronized the *kaliya* befitting their wealth and status. Making this dish in an Instant Pot is like mastering an art form with practice and patience. This recipe will get you a perfect kundan kaliya, which is truly love at first bite. Awadhi cuisine is all about exquisite ingredients such as kewra essence, saffron and gold leaf (edible flakes of gold used for decoration), and the subtle layers of flavor. So, try not to miss these special ingredients when making this meat curry.

9 oz (250 g) bone-in goat meat, cut into 2" (5-cm) pieces

1 tbsp (9 g) white poppy seeds

3 tablespoons (45 ml) hot water, divided

½ tsp saffron threads

2 whole cloves

4 green cardamom pods

1 black cardamom pod

½ tsp ground mace

1 tsp black peppercorns

1 (1" [2.5-cm])-long piece cinnamon stick

½ cup (101 g) ghee, divided

2 cups (320 g) sliced yellow onion

¼ cup (36 g) almonds, skinned

1 tbsp (20 g) ginger and garlic paste

2 tsp (5 g) Kashmiri red chili powder

¼ tsp ground turmeric

1 tsp ground coriander

2 tsp (12 g) salt

½ cup (120 ml) water

½ cup (120 ml) dahi (curd) or plain Greek yogurt, whisked

½ tsp kewra essence

2 edible gold or silver leaves (optional)

Clean and pat dry the meat pieces. Set aside.

Soak the poppy seeds in 2 tablespoons (30 ml) of the hot water. Separately, soak the saffron in the remaining tablespoon (15 ml) of the hot water. Set both aside.

In the Instant Pot set to SAUTÉ mode or in a skillet over medium heat, dry roast the cloves, cardamom pods, mace, peppercorns and cinnamon stick for 40 to 50 seconds, stirring constantly for even roasting and to prevent burning. Then, grind them to a coarse powder using a blender. Set aside in a bowl.

Set the SAUTÉ mode of the Instant Pot for 10 minutes. Add ¼ cup (28 g) of the ghee to the inner pot. Once the ghee is hot, add the onion and fry for 5 to 6 minutes, or until golden and crisp. Reserve half of the fried onion in a bowl and set it aside. Transfer the remaining fried onion to the same blender that was used for the whole spices. Grind to a smooth paste along with the skinned almonds and soaked poppy seeds and their liquid. Set the paste aside.

Set the SAUTÉ mode for 20 minutes. Add the remaining ghee. Add the ginger and garlic paste, red chili powder, turmeric, coriander and meat. Sear the meat pieces until lightly browned and starting to release their juices, 5 to 6 minutes.

Add the prepared onion paste, plus the salt and water. Close the lid. Set the steam valve to the sealing position. Pressure cook at high pressure for 20 minutes. Wait for the natural release of steam.

Add the whisked dahi, whole spice powder, saffron along with its liquid and the kewra essence, and simmer in SAUTÉ mode for 10 minutes, stirring at regular intervals to prevent burning. Garnish with the gold or silver leaves to serve.

NOTE:

✤ Alternatively, you can slow cook the meat. Follow the recipe as suggested, but instead of pressure cooking for 20 minutes, set the SLOW COOK mode for 5 hours.

DAL GOSHT

Lamb and Legumes Curry

Lamb meat cooked with lentils is called *dal gosht* in the Indian subcontinent. The dish is considered nourishing, wholesome and definitely rich in protein. The legumes give the creamy texture to the curry and the meat makes it so delicious. It is also like a one-pot meal, thanks to Instant Pot, that you can enjoy without any sides. But if you prefer sides with this curry, then light Indian breads, such as roti, or steamed basmati rice will be the perfect choice.

SERVES 2

Gluten Free

Clean and pat dry the meat pieces. Set aside.

Rinse the pigeon peas and lentils until the water runs clear. Soak them in water for 15 minutes.

Set the SAUTÉ mode of the Instant Pot for 20 minutes.

Add the ghee to the inner pot. Once the ghee is hot, add the caraway seeds and red onion. Fry the onion for 4 to 5 minutes, or until lightly browned. Add the ginger and garlic paste. Fry for 40 to 50 seconds, or until the raw smell wafts away.

Add the tomato, salt, red chili powder and turmeric, and sauté for 2 to 3 minutes, or until the tomato is mashed up. Add the goat meat. Sauté for the next 5 minutes to sear the meat.

Drain all the water from the soaked legumes. Add them to the inner pot. Stir to mix.

Add the water and mix. Close the lid. Set the steam valve to the sealing position. Pressure cook at high pressure for 20 minutes. Wait for the natural release of steam.

Add the garam masala and ginger, and let the curry simmer in SAUTÉ mode for 5 minutes.

Meanwhile, prepare the tempering: In a skillet, heat the ghee over medium heat. Add the garlic and fry for 2 minutes, or until lightly golden.

Add the red chiles and curry leaves, and fry for 10 seconds. Turn off the heat.

Pour this tempering over the dal gosht just before serving.

Garnish with the mint leaves. Serve warm with bread of your choice.

7 oz (200 g) bone-in goat meat, cut into 2" (5-cm) pieces

¼ cup (43 g) dried split pigeon peas (toor dal)

¼ cup (45 g) dried pink lentils (masoor dal)

4 tbsp (55 g) ghee

1 tsp caraway seeds

1 cup (160 g) sliced red onion

1 tbsp (20 g) ginger and garlic paste

½ cup (90 g) chopped tomato

2 tsp (7 g) salt

1 tsp red chili powder

1 tsp ground turmeric

2 cups (480 ml) water

1 tsp garam masala

1 tbsp (5 g) julienned fresh ginger

5 to 6 mint leaves, chopped, for garnish

TEMPERING (TADKA)

2 tbsp (28 g) ghee

1 tbsp (10 g) chopped garlic

2 dried red chiles

5 to 6 curry leaves

MUTTON KULAMBU

South India–Style Mutton Curry

If you travel across the southern state of Tamil Nadu or visit Sri Lanka, it is inevitable to come across the word *kulambu*, a.k.a. *kuzhambu*. This is a spicy, sour, thin curry made with either vegetables, chicken, seafood or mutton. There are many versions of the kulambu in Tamil cuisine. Staying in southern India for a few years has taught me a trick or two to make a lip-smacking, flavorful kulambu in an Instant Pot.

9 oz (250 g) bone-in lamb, cut into 2" (5-cm) pieces

1 tsp cumin seeds

1 tsp fennel seeds

1 tbsp (5 g) coriander seeds

4 dried red chiles (or to taste)

¼ cup (21 g) grated coconut

6 tbsp (83 g) coconut oil or (90 ml) mustard oil

1 bay leaf

4 whole cloves

4 green cardamom pods

5 to 6 curry leaves

1 cup (160 g) roughly chopped shallots (sambar onion)

1 tbsp (5 g) finely minced fresh ginger

1 tbsp (10 g) finely minced garlic

1 cup (180 g) finely chopped tomato

1 tsp tamarind paste

2 tsp (12 g) salt

¼ tsp red chili powder

1 tsp ground turmeric

½ cup (120 ml) water

2 tbsp (2 g) chopped fresh cilantro, for garnish

Clean and pat dry the meat pieces. Set aside.

In the Instant Pot set to SAUTÉ mode or in a skillet over medium heat, dry roast the cumin, fennel and coriander seeds, red chiles and coconut for 40 to 50 seconds, stirring constantly for even roasting and to prevent burning. Then, grind to a coarse powder, using a spice grinder. Set aside in a bowl.

Set the SAUTÉ mode of the Instant Pot for 20 minutes.

Add the oil to the inner pot. Once the oil is hot, add the bay leaf, cloves, cardamom pods and curry leaves and sauté for 20 to 30 seconds. Add the shallot and fry for 3 to 4 minutes, or until lightly golden.

Add the ginger and garlic, and sauté for 1 minute. Next, add the tomato, tamarind paste, salt, red chili powder, turmeric and prepared spice blend. Sauté for 2 to 3 minutes, or until the tomato is completely mashed.

Add the meat and sauté until the timer beeps. Add the water and stir to mix.

Close the lid. Set the steam valve to the sealing position. Pressure cook at high pressure for 25 minutes. Wait for the natural release of steam.

Open the lid. Simmer the curry in SAUTÉ mode for 5 minutes, stirring at regular intervals. Remove and discard the bay leaf before serving.

Garnish with the cilantro. Serve with rice.

KOSHA MANGOSHA

Bengali-Style Slow Cooker Mutton Curry

Kosha mangosha is a treat for one's culinary senses and comes from the region of Bengal. *Kosha* is the Bengali term for the braising technique, whereas *mangosha* is the word for the meat. The highlights of this curry are the perfectly braised, deep brown masala coating and the slow-cooked meat. It is one of the most popular Bengali festive foods best enjoyed with *basanti pulao* (sweet saffron rice).

Clean and pat dry the meat pieces. Set aside.

Prepare the marinade: In a blender, blend the chopped red onion, dahi, turmeric and red chili powder to a smooth paste. Coat the meat with the paste. Marinate, covered, in the refrigerator overnight or for at least for 1 hour.

Prepare the gravy: Set the SAUTÉ mode of the Instant Pot for 30 minutes. Add the oil to the inner pot. Once the oil is hot, add the cardamom pods, cloves, bay leaf and cinnamon stick, and fry for 10 to 20 seconds.

Add the sliced red onion and fry for 4 to 5 minutes, or until golden. Add the ginger and garlic paste along with a tablespoon (15 ml) of the water. Sauté for 1 minute, or until the onion is deeply browned.

Next, add the marinated meat. Sauté the meat for 5 minutes, or until lightly browned on all sides. Add the whisked dahi, coriander, cumin, red chili powder, salt and sugar, and start the braising process. Keep on sautéing the meat until the timer beeps.

If the masala is sticking to the pot, add 1 to 2 tablespoons (15 to 30 ml) of water while braising. You will notice that the color of curry will change from pale brown to deep brown.

Add the remaining water. Stir to mix nicely. Set the Instant Pot to SLOW COOK mode for 2 hours.

At the 2-hour point, it should be well done. Add the garam masala, ghee, green chiles and cilantro. Simmer in SAUTÉ mode for 10 minutes. Remove and discard the bay leaf before serving.

Serve with yellow rice.

NOTE:

❋ Alternatively, you can cook this in the PRESSURE COOK mode. Follow the recipe instructions as written, but instead of slow cooking for 2 hours, pressure cook the curry at high pressure for 20 minutes. Wait for the natural release of the steam before proceeding.

9 oz (250 g) bone-in goat meat, cut into 2" (5-cm) pieces

MARINADE

1 cup (160 g) chopped red onion

½ cup (120 ml) dahi (curd) or plain Greek yogurt

1 tsp ground turmeric

½ tsp red chili powder

GRAVY

4 tbsp (60 ml) mustard oil

4 green cardamom pods

4 whole cloves

1 bay leaf

1 (1" [2.5-cm])-long piece cinnamon stick

1 cup (160 g) sliced red onion

1 tbsp (20 g) ginger and garlic paste

1 cup (240 ml) water, divided

¼ cup (60 ml) dahi (curd) or plain Greek yogurt, whisked

1 tsp ground coriander

1 tsp ground cumin

2 tsp (5 g) red chili powder

2 tsp (12 g) salt

1 tsp sugar

1 tsp garam masala

1 tbsp (14 g) ghee

2 medium-hot green chiles, such as jalapeños, Thai green chiles or serrano peppers, sliced

2 tbsp (2 g) chopped fresh cilantro

MEAT ALOO SALAN

Lamb and Potatoes Curry

I personally love the combination of starchy potatoes in a rustic, robust meat curry. Meat aloo salan is more of an everyday comforting curry that comes together quickly in the PRESSURE COOK mode of an Instant Pot. If, like me, you adore potatoes, then this is a must-try lamb curry for you.

9 oz (250 g) bone-in lamb, cut into 2" (5-cm) pieces

6 tbsp (90 ml) mustard oil, divided

1 cup (160 g) sliced red onion

1 bay leaf

1 tsp caraway seeds

1 cup (160 g) finely chopped red onion

1 tbsp (20 g) ginger and garlic paste

1 tsp red chili powder

1 tsp ground turmeric

1 tsp ground coriander

½ cup (120 ml) dahi (curd) or plain Greek yogurt, whisked

1 cup (240 ml) water

1¼ tsp (7 g) salt

1 cup (170 g) wedge-cut potato

1 tsp garam masala

2 medium-hot green chiles, such as jalapeños, Thai green chiles or serrano peppers, sliced

2 tbsp (2 g) chopped fresh cilantro, for garnish

Clean and pat dry the meat pieces. Set aside.

Set the SAUTÉ mode of the Instant Pot for 20 minutes. Add 4 tablespoons (60 ml) of the oil to the inner pot. Once the oil is hot, add the sliced red onion and fry for 5 minutes, or until crisp and golden. Transfer to a plate.

Add the remaining 2 tablespoons (30 ml) of the oil to the pot. Add the bay leaf, caraway seeds and chopped red onion. Fry until the onion is lightly browned. Add the ginger and garlic paste along with the red chili powder, turmeric and coriander, and sauté for 20 seconds.

Next, add the meat. Sauté for 5 to 6 minutes, or until meat is lightly browned on all sides.

Add the whisked dahi, mix and sauté for 5 minutes, stirring.

Add the water and salt, and mix. Close the lid. Set the steam valve to the sealing position. Pressure cook at high pressure for 15 minutes. Manually release the steam.

Add the potato, garam masala, green chiles and fried onion, and close the lid. Set the steam valve to the sealing position. Pressure cook at high pressure for 5 minutes. Wait for the natural release of the steam. Remove and discard the bay leaf before serving.

Garnish with the cilantro. Serve with your flatbread of choice.

Keema Kaleji Curry

Ground Goat Meat and Liver Curry

This is a truly Punjabi-style curry. You will be surprised to know that liver is very commonly eaten across India. It is added to a variety of meat curries, and also used as a key ingredient in many dishes. The combination of ground meat and liver is heavenly, and when cooked in a spicy masala, it becomes irresistible. Do not forget to sprinkle fresh cilantro on top of the curry for a refreshing taste.

SERVES 2

Gluten Free

✤

Place the liver in a strainer. Rinse well with water. Set aside.

In a blender, make a coarse paste of 2 of the green chiles, the ginger and garlic, using 1 to 2 tablespoons (15 to 30 ml) of water.

Set the SAUTÉ mode of the Instant Pot for 20 minutes.

Add the oil to the inner pot. Once the oil is smoking hot, add the cardamom pod and caraway seeds, and fry for 10 to 20 seconds. Add the red onion and fry for 5 minutes, or until golden.

Add the prepared green chile paste along with a tablespoon (15 ml) of water. Sauté for 1 minute

Add the tomato, red chili powder, turmeric, coriander and salt. Sauté until the tomato completely breaks down and turns into a mash, 3 to 5 minutes.

Add the liver and sauté for 1 minute. Add the ground meat and sauté the meat for 5 minutes, or until it is lightly browned.

Add the whisked dahi and mix nicely with the meat. Sauté until the timer beeps. Add the ½ cup (120 ml) of water and mix. Close the lid. Set the steam valve to the sealing position. Pressure cook at high pressure for 8 minutes. Wait for the natural release of steam.

Slice the remaining 2 green chiles and add them to the Instant Pot, along with the garam masala, mint leaves and lemon juice, and mix. Simmer in SAUTÉ mode for 2 minutes.

Garnish with the cilantro to serve.

3.5 oz (100 g) goat liver (kaleji)

4 medium-hot green chiles, such as jalapeños, Thai green chiles or serrano peppers, divided

1 (1" [2.5-cm]) piece fresh ginger

4 cloves garlic

½ cup (120 ml) water, plus 2 to 3 tablespoons (30 to 45 ml) for blending and sautéing

4 tbsp (60 ml) mustard oil

1 black cardamom pod, crushed

1 tsp caraway seeds

1 cup (160 g) finely chopped red onion

½ cup (90 g) finely chopped tomato

1 tsp red chili powder

1 tsp ground turmeric

1 tsp ground coriander

1¼ tsp (7 g) salt

9 oz (250 g) ground goat meat (keema)

¼ cup (60 ml) dahi (curd) or plain Greek yogurt, whisked

1 tsp garam masala

1 tbsp chopped fresh mint leaves

2 tbsp (30 ml) fresh lemon juice

2 tbsp (2 g) chopped fresh cilantro, for garnish

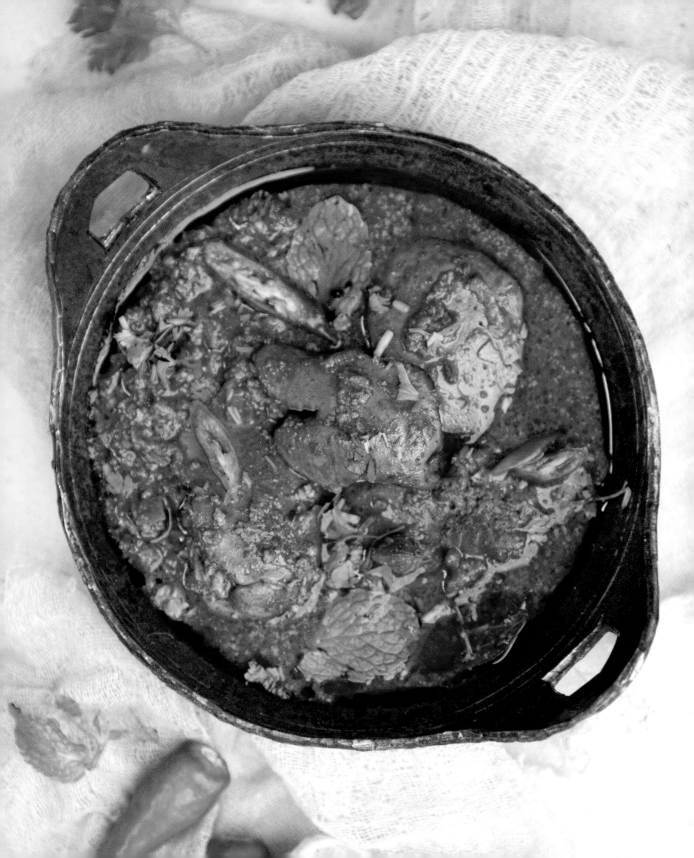

LAMB VEGETABLE KORMA
Slow-Cooked Lamb and Vegetable Korma Curry

This South Indian–style dish was made for the Instant Pot! The creaminess of cashews and coconut, the richness of lamb and the earthiness of vegetables are what make this korma curry so special. It is one of those fridge forage dishes that you can easily make for a weekly curry night—also the best way to sneak vegetables into your family's diet.

9 oz (250 g) boneless lamb, cut into 1½" (4-cm) pieces

¼ cup (35 g) cashews

¼ cup (4 g) fresh cilantro stalks

¼ cup (20 g) desiccated coconut

¼ cup (60 ml) hot water

1 tsp white poppy seeds

1 tsp fennel seeds

1 tbsp (5 g) chopped fresh ginger

2 dried red chiles

6 tbsp (83 g) coconut oil

1 bay leaf

1 black cardamom pod

4 green cardamom pods

6 to 8 curry leaves

1 cup (160 g) finely chopped red onion

1 tbsp (20 g) ginger and garlic paste (see page 231)

½ cup (90 g) finely chopped tomato

1 tsp red chili powder

1 tsp ground turmeric

1¼ tsp (7 g) salt

1 cup (240 ml) water

¼ cup (33 g) diced carrot

¼ cup (43 g) diced potato

¼ cup (25 g) diced green beans

2 medium-hot green chiles, such as jalapeños, Thai green chiles or serrano peppers, sliced

Clean and pat dry the meat pieces. Set aside.

In a blender, make a smooth paste of the cashews, cilantro stalks and coconut, using ¼ cup (60 ml) of hot water. Set aside.

In the Instant Pot set to SAUTÉ mode or in a skillet over low to medium heat, dry roast the poppy seeds, fennel seeds, ginger and dried red chiles for 40 to 50 seconds. A sweet aroma of spices will be released. Make sure they do not start to burn. Then, grind in a spice grinder to a coarse powder.

Set the SAUTÉ mode of the Instant Pot for 20 minutes.

Add the oil to the inner pot. Once the oil is hot, add the bay leaf, cardamom pods and curry leaves. Sauté for 30 to 40 seconds. Add the red onion and fry until it is lightly golden.

Add the tomato, prepared spice powder, red chili powder, turmeric and salt, and sauté for 2 to 3 minutes, or until the tomato breaks down completely.

Add the meat pieces. Sauté until lightly browned on all sides, or for 5 minutes.

Next, add the water and stir to mix. Close the lid. Set the steam valve to the sealing position. Pressure cook at high pressure for 20 minutes. Manually release the steam.

Add the carrot, potato, green beans, prepared cashew paste and green chiles, and stir to combine. Close the lid. Set the steam valve to the sealing position. Pressure cook at high pressure for 2 minutes. Wait for the natural release of steam.

Remove and discard the bay leaf before serving.

Serve with dosa, idli or parotta.

Palak Mutton Rara

Lamb and Spinach Curry

Mutton rara is a unique Indian curry in which two cuts of meat—ground meat (keema) and the bone-in pieces are cooked together in an Instant Pot to create this scrumptious, rustic dish. Today, you can find old classics like this in only a handful of Indian restaurants. The authentic recipe does not call for spinach, but I love the addition of green leaves in this curry. This recipe is spicy, so adjust the quantity of whole spices and masala powders according to your taste.

SERVES 2

Gluten Free

❋

Clean and pat dry the lamb pieces.

In a medium-sized bowl, combine the dahi, ginger and garlic paste, red chili powder, ¼ teaspoon of the turmeric and ½ teaspoon of the salt. Add the lamb and marinate, covered, in the refrigerator for at least 1 hour or better yet overnight.

In a blender, make a smooth paste of the dried red chiles, ginger and garlic, using ¼ cup (60 ml) of hot water. Set aside until you're ready to use it.

Set the SAUTÉ mode of the Instant Pot for 20 minutes.

Add the ghee to the inner pot. Once the ghee is hot, add the bay leaf and cardamom pods. Sauté for 20 seconds. Add the red onion and fry until it is lightly golden.

Add the prepared chile paste, tomato puree, remaining teaspoon of salt, remaining teaspoon of turmeric, coriander and cumin, and sauté for 2 to 3 minutes, or until all the liquid is evaporated.

Add the marinated meat pieces and sauté them until lightly browned on all sides, or for 5 to 6 minutes.

Next, add the ground lamb. Sauté for 5 more minutes. Add the water. Stir to combine.

Close the lid. Set the steam valve to the sealing position. Pressure cook at high pressure for 20 minutes. Wait for the natural release of the steam.

Add the spinach leaves and garam masala, and let the curry simmer in SAUTÉ mode for 5 minutes. Remove and discard the bay leaf before serving.

Garnish with the cilantro. Serve with naan or tandoori roti.

7 oz (200 g) boneless lamb, cut into 1" to 1¼" (2.5- to 3-cm) pieces

½ cup (120 ml) dahi (curd) or plain Greek yogurt

1 tsp ginger and garlic paste

1 tsp red chili powder

1¼ tsp (3 g) ground turmeric, divided

1½ tsp (8 g) salt, divided

4 dried Kashmiri red chiles

1 tbsp (5 g) chopped fresh ginger

1 tbsp (10 g) chopped garlic

¼ cup (60 ml) hot water

4 tbsp (55 g) ghee

1 bay leaf

1 black cardamom pod

4 green cardamom pod

1 cup (160 g) sliced red onion

1 cup (250 g) tomato puree

1 tsp ground coriander

1 tsp ground cumin

3.5 oz (100 g) ground lamb

1 cup (240 ml) water

2 cups (30 g) spinach leaves, chopped

1 tsp garam masala

2 tbsp (2 g) chopped fresh cilantro, for garnish

RAILWAY MUTTON CURRY

Indian Railway Special Meat Curry from British Raj Era

The name of this curry may sound odd at first, but once you know the story behind the title, it makes sense. Once the railway lines were set up during the British Raj, a special menu was developed to serve in the dining car of the trains. Over the decades, one dish in particular became highly popular among the British officers, and it was the railway mutton curry—a spicy masala meat curry toned down with a few splashes of coconut milk. Today, the Indian railway does not serve this curry anymore, but the dish lives in the memoirs of food writers, historians and a handful of curry houses. This Instant Pot version of railways mutton curry is my absolute favorite and totally bookmark worthy!

1 tbsp (5 g) chopped fresh ginger

1 tbsp (10 g) chopped garlic

2 mild green chiles, such as jalapeños, Thai green chiles or serrano peppers

1 cup (240 ml) water, plus 1 to 2 tbsp (15 to 30 ml) for blending (optional)

9 oz (250 g) bone-in lamb, cut into 1½" to 2" (4- to 5-cm) pieces

6 tbsp (90 ml) vegetable oil

1 bay leaf

4 whole cloves

4 green cardamom pods

1 cup (160 g) sliced red onion

1 cup (180 g) finely chopped tomato

1¼ tsp (7 g) salt

1 tsp freshly ground black pepper

1 tsp ground turmeric

½ tsp ground red chili powder

1 tsp ground coriander

1 cup (240 ml) thick coconut milk

2 tbsp (2 g) chopped fresh cilantro, for garnish

In a blender, make a coarse paste of the ginger, garlic, and green chiles, adding 1 to 2 tablespoons (15 to 30 ml) of water (if needed).

Clean and pat dry the meat pieces. Set aside.

Set the SAUTÉ mode of the Instant Pot for 20 minutes.

Add the oil to the inner pot. Once the oil is hot, add the bay leaf, cloves and cardamom pods. Sauté for 20 seconds. Add the red onion and fry until it is lightly golden.

Add the prepared chile paste, tomato, salt, black pepper, turmeric, red chili powder and coriander, and sauté for 2 to 3 minutes, or until the tomato breaks down completely.

Add the meat pieces and sauté them until lightly browned on all sides, or for 5 minutes.

Add the water and mix. Close the lid. Set the steam valve to the sealing position. Pressure cook at high pressure for 20 minutes. Manually release the steam.

Add the coconut milk, and cook in SAUTÉ mode for 5 minutes. Remove and discard the bay leaf before serving.

Garnish with the cilantro and serve.

SAFED MAAS

Lamb in White Sauce

Safed means "white" in Hindi, and *maas* is the term for "meat." Traditionally, this Rajasthani curry was made with wild boar, deer or any catch of the day hunted by the royals. It is a rich, creamy, indulgent dish that will make you fall in love with its taste. Unlike the other vibrant food of Rajasthan, this one has a calming appearance and a mildly spicy taste.

SERVES 2

Gluten Free

Clean and pat dry the meat pieces. Set aside.

In a medium-sized bowl, whisk together the dahi, ginger and garlic paste and 1 teaspoon of the salt until smooth. Marinate the meat in this mixture, covered, in the refrigerator for at least 1 hour or best overnight.

In a blender, make a coarse paste of the cashews, almonds, poppy seeds and peppercorns. Add the lukewarm milk and blend into a smooth paste, adding more milk, if needed. Set aside.

Set the SAUTÉ mode of the Instant Pot for 20 minutes.

Add the ghee to the inner pot. Once the ghee is hot, add the bay leaf, cloves, red chiles and cardamom pods. Sauté for 20 seconds. Add the onion and fry until it is lightly golden.

Add the marinated meat and sauté it for the next 6 minutes, or until it is lightly browned on all sides.

Season with the remaining teaspoon of salt. Add the cashew paste and water. Stir to mix.

Close the lid. Set the steam valve to the sealing position. Pressure cook at high pressure for 20 minutes. Wait for the natural release of steam.

Add the cream. Simmer the curry in SAUTÉ mode for 5 minutes. Remove and discard the bay leaf before serving.

Garnish with the cilantro and serve.

9 oz (250 g) bone-in lamb, cut into 1½" to 2" (4- to 5-cm) pieces

½ cup (120 ml) dahi (curd) or plain Greek yogurt

1 tbsp (20 g) ginger and garlic paste

2 tsp (12 g) salt, divided

2 tbsp (9 g) cashews

2 tbsp (18 g) almonds, skinned

1 tbsp (9 g) white poppy seeds

1 tsp black peppercorns

4 tbsp (60 ml) lukewarm milk, plus more if needed

4 tbsp (55 g) ghee

1 bay leaf

4 whole cloves

4 dried red chiles

4 green cardamom pods

1 cup (160 g) finely chopped white onion

½ cup (120 ml) water

4 tbsp (60 ml) light cream

2 tbsp (2 g) chopped fresh cilantro, for garnish

MEAT KI KADHI

Lamb Cooked in Gram Flour and Yogurt Curry

The vibrant state of Rajasthan is well known for its hospitality and food. The variety of vegetarian and meat dishes in Rajasthani cuisine is extensive. One lost recipe from the state is meat ki kadhi, a spicy, sour lamb cooked in a gram flour and yogurt sauce. Kadhi is a popular Indian vegetarian stew. The addition of meat to the kadhi gives it a whole new, delicious dimension.

6 cloves garlic

2 mild green chiles, such as jalapeños, Thai green chiles or serrano peppers, chopped

¼ cup (4 g) fresh cilantro stalks

1 cup (240 ml) water, plus 1 to 2 tbsp (15 to 30 ml) for blending

9 oz (250 g) bone-in lamb, cut into 1½" to 2" (4- to 5-cm) pieces

6 tbsp (90 ml) oil

1 bay leaf

4 whole cloves

4 dried red chiles, such as Kashmiri

¼ tsp asafetida

1 tbsp (5 g) grated fresh ginger

1 cup (160 g) sliced red onion

¼ cup (45 g) finely chopped tomato

1 tsp red chili powder

1 tsp ground turmeric

1¼ tsp (7 g) salt

1 cup (240 ml) dahi (curd) or plain Greek yogurt

½ cup (60 g) gram (chickpea) flour

2 tbsp (2 g) chopped fresh cilantro, for garnish

In a blender, make a fine paste of the garlic, green chiles and cilantro stalks, using 1 to 2 tablespoons (15 to 30 ml) of water.

Clean and pat dry the meat pieces. Set aside.

Set the SAUTÉ mode of the Instant Pot for 20 minutes.

Add the oil to the inner pot. Once the oil is hot, add the bay leaf, cloves, red chiles, asafetida and ginger. Sauté for 20 seconds. Add the red onion and fry until it is lightly golden.

Add the tomato, prepared chile paste, red chili powder and turmeric, and sauté for 2 to 3 minutes, or until the tomato breaks down completely.

Add the meat and sauté it for the next 6 minutes, or until it is lightly browned on all sides.

Season with the salt. Add the cup (240 ml) of water and mix. Close the lid. Set the steam valve to the sealing position. Pressure cook at high pressure for 15 minutes. Wait for the natural release of steam.

In a small bowl, whisk together the dahi and gram flour to make a smooth, lump-free batter.

Add the batter slowly to the inner pot, constantly stirring clockwise to mix.

Close the lid. Set the steam valve to the sealing position. Cook in SOUP mode for 10 minutes. Wait for the steam to release naturally. Remove and discard the bay leaf before serving.

Garnish with the chopped cilantro. Serve with rice.

FRESH FROM THE SEA

With a coastline of 4,660 miles (7,500+ km), nine coastal states sharing boundaries with the sea, in addition to many rivers crisscrossing the inland area, seafood has been part of Indian cuisine since ancient times. So, when the French came to India for trade, far from their homeland, they found comfort in the Indian seafood around such coastal towns as Pondicherry, Daman, Diu and Goa. And so did the Portuguese and Dutch.

Until I reached the age of 30, I was not fond of seafood. The only kind I knew was Himalayan trout that, too, was never cooked in my mother's pure vegetarian kitchen. I was okay with eating fish only in the form of pakora (Indian fritters), covered with a thick gram flour batter.

My relationship with seafood changed after moving to one of India's most popular coastal cities—Madras (now called Chennai). Thus, the journey of a seafood explorer started, and there was no turning back. Today, I love it more than chicken or red meat.

When it comes to modern-day Indian seafood curries, you can see the confluence of European-style cooking and local ingredients. The reason behind that is from the early days, when the Portuguese, Dutch, French and the British all tried to control the major ports and coastal cities of India for business trade. Hence, their style of cooking influenced the communities of that particular coastal region. And there begins the journey of modern-day fish and seafood curries. But, of course, many traditional-style seafood curries are still made with great pride in each coastal region of India.

During the colonial era, Indian fish curries, such as Meen Molly (page 193), were curated to cater to the taste buds of Europeans; whereas Goan-Style Prawn Caldinho (page 152) exemplifies Portuguese and coastal fusion flavors.

In this chapter, you will find some of my favorite seafood curries from different regions of India, which you can cook to perfection with ease—and in a shorter period of time—in an Instant Pot. Don't beat yourself up about finding the exact variety of fish suggested in the recipe. It is always best to find a local substitute. At least, that is how I work around fish recipes from other parts of the world.

GOAN-STYLE PRAWN CALDINHO

Yellow Shrimp Curry in a Sweet and Spicy Sauce

In Goa, you will find fiery red vindaloo curry, refreshing green *cafreal masala* and *xacuti* curry, and then there is bright yellow *caldinho* curry. The Portuguese influence in the Goan cuisine is very evident, as in this caldinho curry and its name. This is a mildly spicy, subtle, soupy prawn curry.

Clean and devein the prawns. Leave the tails intact.

In a medium-sized bowl, marinate the prawns with ½ teaspoon of the turmeric, ½ teaspoon of the salt and all the vinegar. Set aside while you prepare the curry.

In the Instant Pot set to SAUTÉ mode or in a skillet over medium heat, dry roast the coconut, cumin seeds, peppercorns, mild green chiles and garlic for 30 to 40 seconds. Transfer to a blender and blend into a paste along with 1 tablespoon (1 g) of the cilantro, using 1 to 2 tablespoons (15 to 30 ml) of water. Set this curry paste aside.

Set the SAUTÉ mode of the Instant Pot for 15 minutes.

Add the oil to the inner pot. Once the oil is hot, add the curry leaves and red onion. Fry until the onion is lightly golden.

Add the tomato, tamarind paste, remaining teaspoon of turmeric and remaining teaspoon of salt, and sauté for 2 to 3 minutes, or until the tomato is mashed up.

Add the prepared curry paste along with the marinated prawns. Sauté for 1 minute, or until the prawns turn light pink.

Add the water and mix. Close the lid. Set the steam valve to the sealing position. Pressure cook at low pressure for 2 minutes. Wait for the natural release of steam.

Add the coconut milk, sliced green chiles and remaining 2 tablespoons (2 g) of chopped cilantro. Simmer the curry in SAUTÉ mode for 2 minutes.

Serve with rice for a delicious curry night.

NOTE:

❊ Alternatively, you can make this curry with butterfish, tilapia, snapper or white pomfret.

9 oz (250 g) king prawns, peeled (see note)

1½ tsp (3 g) ground turmeric, divided

1½ tsp (9 g) salt, divided

1 tbsp (15 ml) malt vinegar or white wine vinegar

1 tbsp (5 g) chopped coconut

1 tsp cumin seeds

1 tsp black peppercorns

2 mild green chiles, such as jalapeños, Thai green chiles or serrano peppers, chopped

4 cloves garlic

3 tbsp (3 g) chopped fresh cilantro, divided

¼ cup (60 ml) water, plus 1 to 2 tbsp (15 to 30 ml) for blending

4 tbsp (55 g) coconut oil

5 to 6 curry leaves

1 cup (160 g) finely chopped red onion

⅓ cup (60 g) finely chopped tomato

1 tsp tamarind paste

½ cup (120 ml) thick coconut milk

2 medium-hot green chiles, such as jalapeños, Thai green chiles or serrano peppers, sliced

CRAB MASALA CURRY

Whole Crab Curry

After moving to Chennai (formerly Madras), I have fallen in love with seafood, and in particular with crab. It is so juicy, tender, fibrous and perfect for absorbing the flavors of a curry. This is a typical Madras-style crab curry with loads of spices that you can make with ease in an Instant Pot. One bite and it's pure ambrosia. If you are not comfortable with using a whole crab for the curry, use fresh or frozen crabmeat.

1 (9-oz [250-g]) crab with shell

1 tsp coriander seeds

1 tsp cumin seeds

1 tsp fennel seeds

1 tsp black peppercorns

4 dried red chiles

6 shallots (sambar onion)

1 tbsp (5 g) grated fresh ginger

1 tbsp (10 g) chopped garlic

½ cup (42 g) grated coconut

1 cup (240 ml) water, plus 4 tbsp (60 ml) for blending

6 tbsp (84 g) coconut oil

1 tsp black mustard seeds

8 curry leaves

1 cup (160 g) finely chopped red onion

½ cup (90 g) finely chopped tomato

1 tbsp (15 g) tamarind paste

1 tsp ground turmeric

1 tsp red chili powder

1¼ tsp (7 g) salt

2 mild to medium-hot green chiles, such as jalapeños, Thai green chiles or serrano peppers, sliced

2 tbsp (2 g) chopped fresh cilantro

Clean the crab, then set aside.

In the Instant Pot set to SAUTÉ mode or in a skillet over medium heat, dry roast the coriander, cumin and fennel seeds, peppercorns, red chiles, shallots, ginger and garlic for 1 minute. Transfer to a blender. Dry roast the coconut for 30 to 40 seconds. Transfer to the same blender as the roasted spices, and blend everything to a smooth paste, using 4 tablespoons (60 ml) of water. Set this curry paste aside.

Set the SAUTÉ mode of the Instant Pot for 20 minutes.

Add the oil to the inner pot. Once the oil is hot, add the mustard seeds, curry leaves and red onion. Sauté until the onion is lightly browned, 3 to 4 minutes.

Add the tomato, tamarind paste, turmeric and red chili powder, and sauté for the next 2 to 3 minutes, or until the tomato breaks down.

Add the crab and prepared curry paste, and sauté for 5 minutes.

Add the cup (240 ml) of water and salt, and mix. Close the lid. Set the steam valve to the venting position. Set the Instant Pot to SLOW COOK mode for 30 minutes. Wait for the natural release of the steam. Add the green chiles and cilantro before serving and enjoy.

PRAWN DO PYAZA
Punjabi-Style Shrimp and Shallots Curry

Do pyaza–style curries are the hot favorite in Indian restaurants. There are many folktales around the creation of this curry. As far as I am concerned, I love do pyaza for its rustic taste, texture and the crunch of extra onions in the gravy. The juicy prawns, cooked in a spicy Punjabi-style gravy with two types of onion—red onion and shallots (sambar onion), come top in my favorite Instant Pot curry lists.

Clean and devein the prawns. Leave the tails intact.

In a medium-sized bowl, marinate the prawns with the ginger and garlic paste, ½ teaspoon of the turmeric, ½ teaspoon of the red chili powder and ¼ teaspoon of the salt. Set aside while you prepare the curry.

In a mortar and pestle or spice grinder, grind the cumin seeds, coriander seeds and dried red chiles to a coarse powder. Set aside.

Set the SAUTÉ mode of the Instant Pot for 15 minutes.

Add the oil to the inner pot. Once the oil is smoking hot, add the onion and fry for 3 to 4 minutes or until lightly browned.

Add the tomato, ground coriander, remaining teaspoon of salt, remaining teaspoon of turmeric and remaining teaspoon of red chili powder, and sauté for 2 to 3 minutes, or until the tomato breaks down completely.

Add the marinated prawns. Sauté for 1 minute, or until they turn light pink.

Add the water and mix. Close the lid. Set the steam valve to the sealing position. Pressure cook at low pressure for 2 minutes. Wait for the natural release of steam.

Set the SAUTÉ mode for 5 minutes. Add the whisked dahi, shallots, bell pepper, prepared spice blend, garam masala, fenugreek leaves and green chiles. Simmer for 5 minutes to soften the bell pepper and thicken the sauce.

Garnish with the cilantro and serve.

9 oz (250 g) prawns, peeled

1 tbsp (20 g) ginger and garlic paste

1½ tsp (3 g) ground turmeric, divided

1½ tsp (4 g) red chili powder, divided

1¼ tsp (7 g) salt, divided

1 tsp cumin seeds

1 tsp coriander seeds

2 dried red chiles

4 tbsp (60 ml) mustard oil

½ cup (80 g) finely chopped yellow onion

1 cup (250 g) pureed tomato

1 tsp ground coriander

¼ cup (60 ml) water

¼ cup (60 ml) dahi (curd) or plain Greek yogurt, whisked

½ cup (80 g) shallots (sambar onion), large ones cut in half

½ cup (75 g) seeded and diced green bell pepper

1 tsp garam masala

1 tsp dried fenugreek leaves (kasuri methi)

2 mild green chiles, such as jalapeños, Thai green chiles or serrano peppers, sliced

1 tbsp (1 g) chopped fresh cilantro, for garnish

FRIED FISH CURRY

Crispy Fish Filet in a Spicy Masala Sauce

A crispy, panfried filet of fish dunked in a flavorful curry is a truly delicious delight. Rohu, catla, Asian carp, pollock or any other meaty, firm and flavorsome fish is the perfect choice for this curry. This dish tastes exceptional with white rice. And it gets ready in no time in an Instant Pot.

4 cloves garlic

1 (1" [2.5-cm]) piece fresh ginger

2 dried red chiles

1 tsp coriander seeds

1¼ tsp (2 g) ground turmeric, divided

1¼ tsp (7 g) salt, divided

½ cup (120 ml) water, plus 1 to 2 tbsp (15 to 30 ml) for blending

9 oz (250 g) fish filet, cut into steaks

6 tbsp (90 ml) vegetable oil, divided

1 tsp black mustard seeds

6 to 8 curry leaves

½ cup (80 g) finely chopped red onion

1 tsp ground coriander

½ tsp red chili powder

1 tbsp (15 g) tamarind paste

4 tbsp (60 ml) thick coconut milk

In a blender, make a smooth paste of the garlic, ginger, dried red chiles, coriander seeds, ¼ teaspoon of the turmeric and ¼ teaspoon of the salt, using 1 to 2 tablespoons (15 to 30 ml) of water. Transfer the masala paste to a medium-sized bowl.

Marinate the fish filet with the masala paste, covered, in the refrigerator for 30 minutes. Set aside.

Set the SAUTÉ mode of the Instant Pot for 8 minutes.

Add 4 tablespoons (60 ml) of the oil to the inner pot. Once the oil is hot, arrange the marinated fish filet in the inner pot. Cook for 4 minutes on each side, or until crisp on both sides. Transfer to a plate.

Set the SAUTÉ mode for 15 minutes. Add the remaining 2 tablespoons (30 ml) of oil to the inner pot.

Add the mustard seeds and curry leaves. Once the seeds splutter, add the red onion and fry for 3 to 4 minutes, or until it is browned.

Add the remaining teaspoon of turmeric, remaining teaspoon of salt, coriander and red chili powder, and sauté for 30 to 40 seconds.

Next, add the tamarind paste, ½ cup (120 ml) of water and the coconut milk, and simmer the curry for 5 minutes to thicken the sauce. At last, add the fried fish, cover the inner pot with the glass lid and simmer for 2 to 3 minutes for the fish to absorb the flavor of the curry.

Serve with rice.

SERVES 2

Gluten Free

✻

1 cup (180 g) diced tomato

4 cloves garlic

1 (1" [2.5-cm]) piece fresh ginger

2 mild green chiles, such as jalapeños, Thai green chiles or serrano peppers, chopped

¼ cup (4 g) cilantro stalks

1¼ cups (300 ml) water, divided

4 tbsp (60 ml) mustard oil

1 tsp nigella seeds

1 tsp fennel seeds

1 tsp red chili powder

1 tsp ground turmeric

1 tsp ground coriander

1¼ tsp (7 g) salt

¼ tsp garam masala

9 oz (250 g) white fish filet, cut into steaks (see note)

2 tbsp (2 g) chopped fresh cilantro, for garnish

TOMATO FISH CURRY

White Fish Poached in a Tomato Gravy

If you are looking for light, subtly spicy Indian fish curry, then I highly recommend trying this recipe. It is nothing but a delicate filet of white fish poached in a flavorful tomato curry sauce using the SAUTÉ mode of an Instant Pot. It tastes delicious with aromatic basmati rice.

In a blender, blend the tomato, garlic, ginger, green chiles and cilantro stalks to a smooth paste, using ¼ cup (60 ml) of the water. Set aside.

Set the SAUTÉ mode of the Instant Pot for 20 minutes.

Add the oil to the inner pot. Once the oil is hot, add the nigella and fennel seeds, and sauté for 20 seconds.

Add the blended curry paste, red chili powder, turmeric, coriander and salt, and sauté for 5 minutes. The masala should start sticking to the pot.

Add the remaining cup (240 ml) of water and the garam masala. Stir to mix. Once the curry starts to bubble, gently add the fish filet. Cover the pot with the glass lid. Simmer for 4 to 5 minutes, or until the fish is fully cooked.

Garnish with the cilantro.

NOTE:

✻ Basa, cod, haddock, tilapia or any other similar white, buttery fish is the perfect choice for this curry.

Prawn Drumstick Curry

Kerala-Style Shrimp Curry with Drumsticks

This is a simple, comforting and nourishing prawn curry from South India. Drumstick is the stem of a moringa plant. It is a vegetable commonly found in Asia and has nothing to do with chicken drumsticks. The moringa plant is the New Age superfood and tastes like a toned-down version of matcha. For centuries in South Indian cuisine, drumsticks have been added to curries, stews, one-pot meals and chutneys. Many Indian grocery stores abroad have started to stock drumsticks and moringa leaves because of their high demand.

SERVES 2

Gluten Free

In the Instant Pot set to SAUTÉ mode or in a skillet over medium heat, dry roast the coconut, coriander seeds, fennel seeds and red chiles for 30 to 40 seconds. Transfer to a blender and blend into a smooth paste, using 1 to 2 tablespoons (15 to 30 ml) of water. Set aside.

Clean and devein the prawns. Leave the tails intact.

In a medium-sized bowl, coat the prawns with ½ teaspoon of the turmeric, ½ teaspoon of the red chili powder and ¼ teaspoon of the salt and chill, covered, in the refrigerator for 30 minutes.

Set the SAUTÉ mode of the Instant Pot for 15 minutes.

Add the oil to the inner pot. Once the oil is hot, add the mustard seeds, curry leaves and red onion. Fry until the onion is lightly browned. Add the ginger and garlic paste. Sauté for 40 to 50 seconds.

Add the tomato, remaining teaspoon of turmeric, remaining teaspoon of red chili powder and remaining teaspoon of salt, and sauté for 2 to 3 minutes.

Add the spice-coated prawns and drumstick. Sauté for 2 minutes, or until the prawns become light pink. Add the ¼ cup (60 ml) of water and mix.

Close the lid. Set the steam valve to the sealing position. Pressure cook at high pressure for 2 minutes. Wait for the natural release of steam.

Garnish with curry leaves.

¼ cup (42 g) grated coconut

1 tbsp (5 g) coriander seeds

½ tsp fennel seeds

2 dried red chiles

¼ cup (60 ml) water, plus 1 to 2 tbsp (15 to 30 ml) for blending

9 oz (250 g) prawns, peeled

1½ tsp (3 g) ground turmeric, divided

1½ tsp (4 g) red chili powder, divided

1¼ tsp (7 g) salt, divided

4 tbsp (55 g) coconut oil

1 tsp black mustard seeds

6 to 8 curry leaves, plus more for garnish

1 cup (160 g) finely chopped red onion

1 tbsp (20 g) ginger and garlic paste

½ cup (125 g) pureed tomato

1 cup (150 g) sliced drumstick, cleaned and cut into ½" (1.3-cm) pieces (see note)

NOTE:

❈ Select tender drumstick stems/pods so that they take less time to cook.

SERVES 2

Gluten Free

❋

CHINGRI MALAI CURRY

Bengali-Style Creamy Shrimp Curry

The word *chingri* means "prawns" in Bengali and the word *malai* describes the buttery texture of the curry. This is a Bengali-style smooth, creamy coconut milk–flavored curry made with king or tiger prawns. You can make it with medium-sized prawns as well.

1 cup (160 g) chopped onion

1 tbsp (5 g) chopped ginger

2 dried red chiles

1 to 2 tablespoons (15 to 30 ml) water, for blending

9 oz (250 g) king prawns, peeled

1½ tsp (3 g) ground turmeric, divided

1 tsp salt, plus a pinch

4 tbsp (60 ml) vegetable oil

1 bay leaf

1 (1" [2.5-cm])-long piece cinnamon stick

4 green cardamom pods

1 tsp red chili powder

1 cup (240 ml) coconut milk, divided

¼ cup (60 ml) dahi (curd) or plain Greek yogurt, whisked

1 tsp garam masala

2 medium-hot green chiles, such as jalapeños, Thai green chiles or serrano peppers, sliced

4 tbsp (60 ml) coconut cream

In a blender, make a paste of the onion, ginger and dried red chiles, using 1 to 2 tablespoons (15 to 30 ml) of water.

Clean and devein the prawns. Leave the tails intact. Coat the prawns with ½ teaspoon of the turmeric and a pinch of salt.

Set the SAUTÉ mode of the Instant Pot for 30 minutes.

Add the oil to the inner pot. Once the oil is hot, add the prawns and fry for 1 minute on each side. Transfer to a plate.

To the same oil, add the bay leaf, cinnamon stick and cardamom pods, and fry for 20 seconds.

Add the prepared onion paste. Fry the masala for the next 5 minutes. Halfway through, add the remaining teaspoon of turmeric, red chili powder and remaining teaspoon of salt. Once the masala starts sticking to the pot, add 1 to 2 tablespoons (15 to 30 ml) of the coconut milk. Do not add all the milk at this time.

Add the whisked dahi. Fry the masala for the next 2 minutes, or until the oil starts oozing from it.

Add the remaining coconut milk. Stir. Once the curry starts to bubble, add the prawns, garam masala and green chiles, and mix. Cover the pot with the lid. Simmer for 5 minutes. Remove and discard the bay leaf.

Add the coconut cream, mix nicely, and serve.

MADRAS MEEN KULAMBU

Spicy Fish Curry from Madras

This is another delicious curry from Madras. The title literally translates to "Madras-style fish curry." It is a spicy, sour, lip-smacking dish flavored with tamarind and a special curry paste. I often make it for our weeknight dinner; in an Instant Pot, it is ready in under 30 minutes. Seer fish, barracuda, snapper, vanjaram or pomfret are perfect choices for this curry recipe. Adjust the number of chiles per personal preference or add a splash of coconut milk to balance the heat.

SERVES 2

Gluten Free

In a medium-sized bowl, coat the fish filets with ½ teaspoon of the turmeric, ½ teaspoon of the red chili powder and ½ teaspoon of the salt. Chill, covered, in the refrigerator for 30 minutes.

Set the SAUTÉ mode of the Instant Pot for 2 minutes.

Add 2 tablespoons (30 ml) of the sesame oil to the inner pot. Once the oil is hot, add the cumin, coriander and fennel seeds, black peppercorns, garlic cloves, coconut and dried red chiles. Fry for 40 to 50 seconds. Transfer to a blender and blend into a smooth paste using the oil from the pot.

Set the SAUTÉ mode of the Instant Pot for 30 minutes.

Add the remaining 4 tablespoons (60 ml) of oil to the inner pot. Once the oil is hot, add the mustard seeds, curry leaves and onion. Sauté until the onion becomes tender and translucent, 2 to 3 minutes.

Add the tomato, remaining teaspoon of turmeric, remaining teaspoon of red chili powder, remaining teaspoon of salt, prepared curry paste and tamarind paste. Sauté for the next 5 minutes. Once the masala starts sticking to the pot, add the water. Stir to mix.

Once the curry starts to boil, gently add the spice-coated fish filet. Cover the pot with the glass lid. Cook until the fish is tender, about 5 minutes. Do not cook the fish for too long after adding it to the curry, as it might break apart.

Garnish with the cilantro.

9 oz (250 g) fish, cut into thick steaks

1½ tsp (3 g) ground turmeric, divided

1½ tsp (4 g) red chili powder, divided

1½ tsp (9 g) salt, divided

6 tbsp (90 ml) sesame oil, divided

2 tbsp (12 g) cumin seeds

1 tbsp (5 g) coriander seeds

1 tsp fennel seeds

1 tbsp (5 g) black peppercorns

4 cloves garlic

1 tbsp (5 g) grated coconut

2 dried red chiles

1 tsp black mustard seeds

6 to 8 curry leaves

1 cup (160 g) finely chopped onion

1 cup (180 g) finely chopped tomato

1 tbsp (15 g) tamarind paste

1½ cups (360 ml) water

2 tbsp (2 g) chopped fresh cilantro, for garnish

VEGETABLE FISH CURRY
Mildly Spicy Fish and Vegetables Curry

Nothing tastes better than a delicate fish simmered in a light curry sauce with such vegetables as snow peas, carrot, okra or fresh fennel. This curry is a perfect Instant Pot–friendly summer meal. Cod, salmon, sole or basa will be the right choice of fish for making this stew. Just before serving, sprinkle with fresh cilantro and serve with rice.

9 oz (250 g) fish filet, cut into pieces

1½ tsp (2 g) ground turmeric, divided

1½ tsp red chili powder, divided

1½ tsp (7 g) salt, divided

1 cup (160 g) chopped red onion

4 tbsp (60 ml) mustard oil

1 tsp black mustard seeds

1 tsp cumin seeds

1 tsp fennel seeds

1 tsp nigella seeds

¼ tsp fenugreek seeds

2 dried red chiles

1 tbsp (5 g) minced fresh ginger

1½ cups (360 ml) water, plus 1 to 2 tbsp (15 to 30 ml) if needed

½ cup (90 g) finely chopped tomato

1 tsp ground cumin

1 tsp ground coriander

1 cup (170 g) sliced potato

1 cup (82 g) sliced baby brinjal (eggplants)

1 cup (180 g) snap peas, halved

1 tsp garam masala

2 mild to medium-hot green chiles, such as jalapeños, Thai green chiles or serrano peppers, sliced

2 tbsp (2 g) chopped fresh cilantro, for garnish

In a medium-sized bowl, coat the fish filet with ½ teaspoon of the turmeric, ½ teaspoon of the red chili powder and ½ teaspoon of the salt. Chill, covered, in the refrigerator for 30 minutes.

In a blender, blend the red onion to a smooth paste. Set aside.

Set the SAUTÉ mode of the Instant Pot for 30 minutes.

Add the oil to the inner pot. Once the oil is smoking hot, add the mustard, cumin, fennel, nigella and fenugreek seeds and the dried red chiles. Sauté for 20 to 30 seconds.

Add the onion paste. Sauté for 2 to 3 minutes, or until the mixture turns light brown.

Add the ginger. Sauté for 30 seconds, or until the raw smell wafts away. If the masala is sticking to the pot, add 1 to 2 tablespoons (15 to 30 ml) of water.

Add the tomato, remaining teaspoon of turmeric, remaining teaspoon of red chili powder, remaining teaspoon of salt, and the cumin and coriander, and sauté for 3 to 4 minutes, or until the tomato is completely mashed up.

Add the potato, baby brinjal, snap peas and the 1½ cups (360 ml) of water, and mix. Close the lid. Set the steam valve to the sealing position. Pressure cook at high pressure for 2 minutes. Wait for the natural release of the steam. Add the garam masala and green chiles, and mix.

Set the SAUTÉ mode for 8 minutes. Once the curry starts to boil, gently slide in the fish pieces. Do not stir vigorously. Cover the pot with the glass lid. Cook until the fish is tender.

Garnish with the cilantro and serve with rice.

FISH DAL CURRY

Fish and Yellow Moong Bean Curry

This is a special dish whose dried yellow moong beans combine with the fish to make a delicious curry. The addition of jaggery and tamarind creates a real outburst of flavors, and not to forget its loads of chopped garlic for an extra garlicky kick. Thanks to the Instant Pot, this curry is actually a filling one-pot meal that does not require many side dishes.

In a medium-sized bowl, coat the fish filets with ½ teaspoon of the turmeric, ½ teaspoon of the red chili powder and ½ teaspoon of the salt. Chill, covered, in the refrigerator for 30 minutes.

Set the SAUTÉ mode of the Instant Pot for 20 minutes.

In the Instant Pot set to SAUTÉ mode or in a skillet over medium heat, dry roast the moong beans until aromatic and lightly browned, 3 to 5 minutes. Transfer to a bowl. Rinse them until the water runs clear. Soak in water and set aside.

Add the oil to the inner pot. Once the oil starts to smoke, add the coated fish pieces and fry until crisp on both sides, 2 to 3 minutes per side. Transfer to a plate.

Add the bay leaf, dried red chiles, cumin seeds, garlic and asafetida to the remaining oil. Sauté for 30 to 40 seconds. Add the red onion and fry until lightly browned, 3 to 4 minutes.

Add the tomato, tamarind paste, ground cumin, coriander, remaining teaspoon of red chili powder, remaining teaspoon of turmeric and remaining teaspoon of salt, and sauté for 2 to 3 minutes, or until the tomato breaks down completely.

Drain all the water from the soaked beans. Add them to the inner pot and sauté for 1 minute.

Add the water, green chiles, brown sugar, ghee and garam masala and mix. Close the lid. Set the steam valve to the sealing position. Pressure cook at high pressure for 4 minutes. Wait for the natural release of steam. Taste and add more seasoning, if required.

Set the SAUTÉ mode for 6 minutes. Once the dal starts to bubble, add the fried fish pieces. Gently stir to combine. Cover the pot with the glass lid. When the timer beeps, remove and discard the bay leaf before serving.

Garnish with the cilantro and serve.

9 oz (250 g) fish pieces (see note)

1½ tsp (2 g) ground turmeric, divided

1½ tsp (3 g) red chili powder, divided

1½ tsp (9 g) salt, divided

½ cup (100 g) dried yellow moong beans

4 tbsp (60 ml) mustard oil

1 bay leaf

2 dried red chiles

1 tsp cumin seeds

1 tbsp (10 g) finely chopped garlic

¼ tsp asafetida

½ cup (80 g) finely chopped red onion

¼ cup (45 g) finely chopped tomato

1 tbsp (15 ml) tamarind paste

1 tsp ground cumin

1 tsp ground coriander

1½ cups (360 ml) water

2 mild green chiles, such as jalapeños, Thai green chiles or serrano peppers, sliced

1 tbsp (15 g) light brown sugar or jaggery powder

1 tbsp (14 g) ghee

1 tsp garam masala

2 tbsp (2 g) finely chopped fresh cilantro, for garnish

NOTE:

❋ Alternatively, you can make this curry with fish head.

Doi Chingri

Shrimp in a Light Yogurt Sauce

This is a thick, tasty, not-so-spicy curry. *Doi chingri* is a Bengali-style curry of prawns cooked in a yogurt sauce. It is an easy recipe that does not require tons of ingredients or a lengthy meal prep and cooks effortlessly in an Instant Pot. I often make it for weeknight family dinners.

1 tbsp (5 g) chopped fresh ginger

2 green chiles, such as jalapeños, Thai green chiles or serrano peppers, chopped

1 cup (240 ml) dahi (curd) or plain Greek yogurt, divided

9 oz (250 g) prawns, peeled

1 tsp ground turmeric

1 tsp red chili powder

1 tsp ground cumin

4 tbsp (60 ml) mustard oil

1 bay leaf

2 dried red chiles

4 green cardamom pods

1 cup (160 g) finely chopped red onion

1 tsp salt

1 tsp sugar

¼ cup (60 ml) water

1 tbsp (14 g) ghee

¼ tsp garam masala

2 tbsp (2 g) chopped fresh cilantro

In a blender, make a paste of the ginger and green chiles, using 1 to 2 tablespoons (15 to 30 ml) of the dahi. Set aside.

Clean and devein the prawns. Leave the tails intact.

In a bowl, combine the turmeric, red chili powder and cumin with the remaining dahi and whisk, making sure it becomes smooth, lump free and of spoon-dripping consistency, or else it will curdle in the curry. Set aside.

Set the SAUTÉ mode of the Instant Pot for 15 minutes.

Add the oil to the inner pot. Once the oil is smoking hot, add the bay leaf, dried red chiles and cardamom pods, and sauté for 20 seconds.

Add the red onion and fry for 3 to 4 minutes, or until lightly browned. Add the prepared ginger and chile paste and fry for 30 to 40 seconds.

Add the whisked dahi, salt and sugar, and sauté for the next 2 minutes, or until the dahi is nicely combined with the masala.

Add the prawns. Sauté for 2 minutes, or until they turn pinkish.

Add the water and mix. Close the lid. Set the steam valve to the sealing position. Pressure cook at high pressure for 2 minutes. Release the steam manually.

Add the ghee, garam masala and cilantro, and mix them into the hot curry. Remove and discard the bay leaf before serving.

Serve with rice.

FUSION FLAVORS

The fusion recipes of India deserve a dedicated book of their own. Each fusion recipe in this chapter has a historic tale attached to it. The invaders from Central Asia, the Mughals, European traders, the colonial autocrats, the Chinese migrants in East India, or the Parsi refugees—each of these communities refashioned Indian cuisine according to their liking. Hence, today we have diverse interpretations of Indian cuisine, including curry.

Along with the Portuguese traders came the renowned vindaloo masala that is featured in my Lamb Vindaloo Curry (page 182), the perfect fusion of Indian spices and the Portuguese technique of preserving the meat with vinegar and garlic. During the colonial era with the setup of the railway network to the famous gentlemen's club in Madras, the Indian cooks started simmering the curries with a dash of coconut milk, as in Chicken Ishtu (page 186), the fusion version of English stew; or preparing the bold Madras Lamb Curry (page 178) enjoyed by the British officers at the club.

With the East India Company came the Chinese migrants to work in the leather tanneries of the Tangra region in West Bengal. Ever since then, there has been no turning back when it comes to Indian Chinese fusion cuisine—one of the country's most popular takeaways and street food.

But the major credit to popularize the fusion of Indian flavors goes to the curry houses of Britain; they are reminiscent of the bygone era of colonial cuisine and culture. Over the last 200 to 300 years, we have adapted these fusion flavors wholeheartedly into Indian cuisine as a souvenir of foreigners who once called India their home. Some of these fusion dishes are still popular and a source of pride at restaurants outside of India, whereas others are just lost recipes. So, if you are bored with regular restaurant takeout-style curries, try these fusion classics, and trust me, each one of these dishes will make you fall in love with curry again and again.

MADRAS LAMB CURRY

Anglo Indian–Style Meat Curry

This is a highly popular curry from the British Raj era. The dish is still served in many Indian restaurants and curry houses in Britain. For many years, it was on the menu of the gentlemen's club in Madras (Chennai). This piquant, unique lamb curry, laced with spices and tomato and full of tempting deliciousness, is actually an Anglo Indian version of Mughlai korma. The original recipe suggested the addition of Madras curry powder, but somehow I still cannot come to terms with curry powder. Hence, this recipe, which contains no curry powder, is cooked to perfection in an Instant Pot.

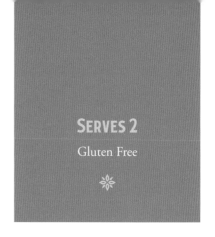

SERVES 2

Gluten Free

✤

Clean and pat dry the meat pieces. Set aside.

In the Instant Pot set to SAUTÉ mode or in a skillet over medium heat, dry roast the coriander, cumin, fennel, poppy and fenugreek seeds, peppercorns, cardamom pods, cloves, cinnamon stick, dried red chiles, ginger and garlic for 1 minute. Transfer to a blender. Dry roast the coconut separately for 50 seconds. Add it to the same blender as the spices. Blend all the ingredients to a smooth paste, using 2 tablespoons (30 ml) of water. Set this masala paste aside.

Set the SAUTÉ mode of the Instant Pot for 15 minutes.

Add the oil to the inner pot. Once the oil is hot, add the bay leaf, curry leaves and shallots. Fry until the shallots become translucent and tender, 2 to 3 minutes.

Add the lamb pieces and sauté for the next 5 minutes, or until they are lightly browned on all sides.

Add the salt, turmeric and red chili powder, and stir to combine. Add the ¼ cup (60 ml) of water and mix. Close the lid. Set the steam valve to the sealing position. Pressure cook at high pressure for 15 minutes. Wait for the natural release of steam.

Add the prepared masala paste and tomato, and stir to mix. Once again, close the lid. Set the steam valve to the sealing position. Pressure cook for 10 minutes. Wait for the natural release of steam. Remove and discard the bay leaf before serving.

Garnish with curry leaves. Serve with dosa or parotta.

NOTE:

✤ This is a medium to highly spicy curry. Reduce the number of chiles and pepper if you want to make it less spicy.

9 oz (250 g) bone-in lamb, cut into 1½" to 2" (4- to 5-cm) pieces

2 tbsp (10 g) coriander seeds

1 tbsp (6 g) cumin seeds

¼ tsp fennel seeds

¼ tsp white poppy seeds

¼ tsp fenugreek seeds

½ tsp black peppercorns

4 green cardamom pods

4 whole cloves

1 (1" [2.5-cm])-long piece cinnamon stick

4 dried red chiles (see note)

1 (1" [2.5-cm]) piece ginger

4 cloves garlic

½ cup (42 g) grated coconut

¼ cup (60 ml) water, plus 2 tbsp (30 ml) for blending

4 tbsp (60 ml) sesame oil

1 bay leaf

8 curry leaves, plus more for garnish

1½ cups (240 g) shallots (sambar onion)

1¼ tsp (7 g) salt

1 tsp ground turmeric

½ tsp red chili powder

½ cup (90 g) chopped tomato

DHANSAK

Parsi-Style Dal and Vegetable Curry

In the western region of Gujarat and Maharashtra, the Parsi influence on local cuisines is evident. *Dhansak* is a fusion delicacy, which combines the Gujarati and Persian styles of cooking. It is a hearty, wholesome, one-pot stew of legumes, vegetables and spices. This vegetarian recipe comes together beautifully in an Instant Pot. You can add your vegetables of choice to the dhansak.

½ cup (85 g) dried split pigeon peas (toor dal)

¼ cup (50 g) dried yellow moong beans

¼ cup (45 g) dried pink lentils (masoor dal)

1 tbsp (5 g) coriander seeds

1 tsp cumin seeds

2 dried red chiles

1 (½" [1.3-cm]-long piece cinnamon stick

4 whole cloves

1 tbsp (5 g) chopped fresh ginger

8 cloves garlic

3 cups (720 ml) water, plus 2 tbsp (30 ml) for blending

¼ cup (10 g) fresh mint leaves

¼ cup (4 g) fresh cilantro leaves

2 green chiles, such as jalapeños, Thai green chiles or serrano peppers, chopped

4 tbsp (55 g) ghee

1 cup (160 g) finely chopped red onion

1 cup (180 g) finely chopped tomato

1¼ tsp (7 g) salt

½ tsp red chili powder

½ tsp ground turmeric

½ cup (41 g) diced purple brinjal (eggplant)

½ cup (70 g) peeled, seeded and diced winter squash

½ cup (85 g) diced potato

1 tbsp (15 ml) fresh lemon juice

2 tbsp (2 g) chopped fresh cilantro, for garnish

Combine the pigeon peas, yellow moong beans and pink lentils in a bowl. Rinse until the water runs clear. Soak in water for 15 minutes.

In the Instant Pot set to SAUTÉ mode or a skillet over medium heat, dry roast the coriander and cumin seeds, red chiles, cinnamon stick, cloves, ginger and garlic for 1 minute. Transfer to a blender and blend into a smooth paste, using 2 tablespoons (30 ml) of water. Transfer to a bowl and set aside. This is paste "A."

Next, in a blender, blend the mint, cilantro leaves and green chiles to a coarse paste without using any water. This is paste "B."

Set the SAUTÉ mode of the Instant Pot for 10 minutes.

Add the ghee to the inner pot. Once the ghee is hot, add the red onion and fry until lightly browned. Add the tomato, salt, red chili powder, turmeric and paste "A." Sauté for the next 2 to 3 minutes.

Drain all the water from the soaked legumes. Add them to the pot along with the brinjal, squash and potato. Stir to mix. Add the 3 cups (720 ml) of water. Stir to mix. Close the lid. Set the steam valve to the sealing position. Pressure cook at high pressure for 10 minutes. Wait for the natural release of the steam.

Add paste "B" and the lemon juice, and stir to mix.

Garnish with the chopped cilantro and serve.

LAMB VINDALOO CURRY

Lamb Cooked in a Spicy Vindaloo Masala

The most famous fusion Indian dishes from Goa—vindaloo—are now a worldwide phenomenon among curry lovers. Vindaloo curry is the amalgam of Portuguese-style cooking and Indian spices. This curry is an adaptation of a Portuguese dish called carne de vinha d'alhos: pork cooked in wine, vinegar and garlic. Today, you will find many versions of vindaloo curry. But my favorite is Instant Pot slow-cooked lamb in a spicy and sour pickle, such as this vindaloo masala.

Clean and pat dry the meat pieces. Set aside.

In the Instant Pot set to SAUTÉ mode or in a skillet over medium heat, dry roast the dried red chiles, ginger, garlic, mustard seeds, cumin seeds, peppercorns, cloves, cardamom pods and cinnamon stick for 3 minutes. Transfer to a blender along with the vinegar, tamarind paste, brown sugar and ½ teaspoon of the salt. Grind to a wet paste, using the 6 tablespoons (90 ml) of hot water.

In a medium-sized bowl, marinate the lamb with the wet paste. Cover and chill in the refrigerator overnight or for at least 2 hours.

Set the SAUTÉ mode of the Instant Pot for 15 minutes.

Add the oil to the inner pot. Once the oil is hot, add the curry leaves and red onion. Fry until the onion becomes lightly browned.

Add the marinated meat and sauté for the next 5 to 6 minutes to sear the meat. Season with the remaining teaspoon of salt.

Add the water. Close the lid. Set the steam valve to the sealing position. Pressure cook at high pressure for 20 minutes. Wait for the natural release of steam.

The lamb vindaloo is ready to serve.

NOTE:

❋ You can slow cook this curry for 5 hours for a more delicious result.

SERVES 2

Gluten Free

❋

9 oz (250 g) bone-in lamb, cut into 1½" to 2" (4- to 5-cm) pieces

6 dried Kashmiri red chiles

1 tbsp (5 g) chopped fresh ginger

6 cloves garlic

1 tsp black mustard seeds

1 tsp cumin seeds

1 tsp black peppercorns

½ tsp ground cloves

4 green cardamom pods

1 (1" [2.5-cm])-long piece cinnamon stick

6 tbsp (90 ml) malt, palm or white wine vinegar

1 tbsp (15 g) tamarind paste

1 tbsp (15 g) light brown sugar or jaggery powder

1½ tsp (9 g) salt, divided

6 tbsp (90 ml) hot water, for blending

4 tbsp (60 ml) vegetable oil

5 to 6 curry leaves

1 cup (160 g) finely chopped red onion

½ cup + 2 tbsp (150 ml) water

CHILLI PANEER

Indian Chinese Fusion Paneer Gravy

It all started in the Tangra Region in Calcutta, West Bengal. The region housed many leather tanneries owned and managed by people of Hakka Chinese origin. Over the years, the area developed into a small Chinatown, and the immigrants started selling their native Chinese dishes made with locally available ingredients. Thus began the journey of Indian Chinese fusion cuisine. Today, Indo-Chinese dishes are available all over India, in street food carts, restaurants and takeaway joints. Chili paneer is an Indian Chinese–style vegetarian main course dish that you can enjoy with fried rice or noodles.

7 oz (200 g) paneer

3 tbsp (24 g) cornstarch, divided

1 tbsp (8 g) all-purpose flour

1 tsp soy sauce

1½ tsp (9 g) salt, divided

¼ tsp freshly ground black pepper

2 cups (480 ml) water, divided

4 dried red chiles

¼ cup (60 ml) hot water

1 (1" [2.5-cm]) piece fresh ginger

4 cloves garlic

¼ cup (40 g) chopped yellow onion

2 tbsp (30 ml) tomato sauce

6 tbsp (90 ml) vegetable oil, divided

1 tbsp (10 g) minced garlic

1 tbsp (5 g) minced fresh ginger

1 cup (160 g) diced white onion

½ cup (75 g) diced green bell pepper

½ cup (75 g) diced red bell pepper

1 tbsp (15 ml) white vinegar

1 tbsp (15 ml) light soy sauce

2 tbsp (7 g) chopped green onion

NOTE:

✤ The chili paste is spicy, so taste it and add to the gravy accordingly. We love spicy food, so we add the entire quantity.

Soak the paneer in lukewarm water for 2 minutes to soften. Cut it into 1-inch (2.5-cm) cubes. In a medium-sized bowl, combine 2 tablespoons (16 g) of the cornstarch with the flour, soy sauce, ½ teaspoon of the salt and the black pepper, and mix. Marinate the paneer cubes in this mixture, covered, in the refrigerator for 30 minutes. Add a tablespoon (15 ml) of the water if the marinade is too thick.

Soak the dried red chiles in the ¼ cup (60 ml) of hot water. Cover and set aside for 5 minutes to soften a bit. Transfer the chiles along with their water to a blender, add in the ginger, garlic, onion and tomato sauce and blend into a smooth paste. Set aside.

Make a paste of the remaining tablespoon (8 g) of cornstarch and 2 tablespoons (30 ml) of the water. Mix nicely to make a lump-free slurry. Set aside until needed.

Set the SAUTÉ mode of the Instant Pot for 15 minutes.

Add 4 tablespoons (60 ml) of the oil to the inner pot. Once the oil is hot, add the marinated paneer cubes. Fry until crisp on all sides, 2 minutes per side. Transfer to a plate.

Add the remaining 2 tablespoons (30 ml) of oil and the minced garlic and ginger, and fry for 40 to 50 seconds.

Add the diced onion and fry for 1 minute, or until it becomes translucent. Add both bell peppers and stir fry for 1 minute. Add the vinegar, soy sauce and prepared chili paste.

Season with the remaining teaspoon of salt. Stir, then simmer for 1 minute.

Add the remaining water and the cornstarch slurry, and stir to combine. Add the fried paneer cubes and mix.

Close the lid. Set the steam valve to the sealing position. Cook in STEW mode for 2 minutes. Wait for the natural release of steam.

Garnish with the green onion. Serve with fried rice.

CHICKEN ISHTU

Kerala-Style Chicken and Vegetable Stew

The word *ishtu* comes from "stew." During the colonial era, the native cooks adapted this recipe to please their British sahibs. A mild, comforting chicken curry with such vegetables as onion, potato, carrot, beans and cauliflower, from Kerala, is the symbol of fusion South Indian and British cuisines. The stew is flavored with the warmth of whole spices, coconut milk and thick coconut cream. But the taste of it is far from spicy and like a warm hug of a good English stew.

Make a coarse paste of ginger and garlic, using a mortar and pestle or blender.

Set the SAUTÉ mode of the Instant Pot for 15 minutes.

Add the oil to the inner pot. Once the oil is hot, add the bay leaf, cloves, cardamom pods, cinnamon stick and black peppercorns, and sauté for 30 to 40 seconds.

Add the ginger-garlic paste to the pot along with the curry leaves. Sauté for 40 seconds.

Next, add the onion and fry until lightly browned.

Add the chicken. Sear the chicken pieces by sautéing for 5 minutes. They will become almost opaque. Add the carrot, potato and green beans, salt, coconut milk and green chiles, and stir to combine.

Close the lid. Set the steam valve to the sealing position. Cook in STEW mode for 6 minutes. Wait for the natural release of steam.

Add the coconut cream and garam masala, and simmer for 2 minutes in SAUTÉ mode. Remove and discard the bay leaf before serving.

Serve with rice, appam or dosa.

1 (1" [2.5-cm]) piece fresh ginger

5 cloves garlic

4 tbsp (55 g) coconut oil

1 bay leaf

4 whole cloves

4 green cardamom pods

1 (½" [1.3-cm])-long piece cinnamon stick

1 tsp black peppercorns

6 to 8 curry leaves

1 cup (160 g) sliced white onion

9 oz (250 g) bone-in chicken, cut into 1¼" to 1½" (3- to 4-cm) pieces

½ cup (55 g) diced carrot

½ cup (85 g) diced potato

½ cup (50 g) diced green beans

1¼ tsp (7 g) salt

1 cup (240 ml) coconut milk

2 green chiles, such as jalapeños, Thai green chiles or serrano peppers, sliced

¼ cup (60 ml) coconut cream

1 tsp garam masala

JARDALU SALLI BOTI
Parsi-Style Chicken and Apricot Curry

Jardalu salli boti is a classic meat curry in which boneless pieces of lamb or goat meat are stewed in a sweet and spicy sauce flavored with apricots (*jardalu*). Before serving, the curry is topped with fried potato matchsticks (*salli*). They are very similar to shoestring potato fries. This dish is reminiscent of the Persian and Iranian influence in Parsi cuisine. The use of dried fruits and nuts in savory dishes is very common in Persian cooking. Apart from dried apricots, you need a bit of patience and an Instant Pot to make this delicious curry.

9 oz (250 g) bone-in goat meat, cut into 1½" to 2" (4- to 5-cm) pieces

1 tbsp (5 g) roughly chopped fresh ginger

4 cloves garlic

2 green chiles, such as jalapeños, Thai green chiles or serrano peppers, chopped

1 tsp cumin seeds

¼ cup (60 ml) dahi (curd) or plain Greek yogurt

6 tbsp (90 ml) vegetable oil

1 bay leaf

1 star anise

1½ cups (240 g) finely chopped yellow onion

1 cup (180 g) canned tomato

4 tbsp (64 g) tomato paste or puree

1 tsp ground turmeric

2 tsp (5 g) red chili powder

1 tbsp (15 g) dark brown sugar or jaggery powder

½ cup (120 ml) water, plus 2 tbsp (30 ml) if needed

1 cup (130 g) dried apricots, halved

1¼ tsp (7 g) salt

1 tbsp (15 ml) malt vinegar

2 tbsp (2 g) chopped fresh cilantro

1 cup (150 g) salli (fried potato sticks), store-bought or homemade (see notes)

Clean and pat dry the meat pieces. Set aside.

In a blender, make a coarse paste of the ginger, garlic, green chiles and cumin seeds. In a bowl, combine the paste with the dahi and add the meat. Cover and chill the marinated meat in the refrigerator overnight or for at least 1 hour.

Set the SAUTÉ mode of the Instant Pot for 15 minutes.

Add the oil to the inner pot. Once the oil is hot, add the bay leaf and star anise, and sauté for 30 to 40 seconds. Add the onion and fry until lightly golden.

Add the canned tomato, tomato paste, turmeric, red chili powder and brown sugar, and sauté the masala for 5 minutes. If it's sticking to the pot, add up to 2 tablespoons (30 ml) of water.

Add the marinated meat. Sauté the meat for the next 5 to 6 minutes.

Once the juices of the meat are released, add the apricots, the ½ cup (120 ml) of water and salt, and stir to combine.

Set the Instant Pot to SLOW COOK for 5 hours. Once the meat is tender, add the vinegar and cilantro.

Simmer in SAUTÉ mode for 5 minutes, stirring at regular intervals, to sauté the meat. Remove and discard the bay leaf.

Top the curry with the salli and serve.

NOTES:

✤ Alternatively, you can cook this in PRESSURE COOK mode. Follow the recipe instructions as suggested. Instead of slow cooking the curry for 5 hours, pressure cook at high pressure for 20 minutes. Wait for the natural release of the steam.

✤ You can make salli at home by deep frying or air frying thinly sliced potato. Or use the ready-made ones available at grocery stores for topping the curry.

CARIL DE GALINHA

Portuguese-Style Chicken Curry

SERVES 2

Gluten Free

✤

Caril is the Portuguese word for "curry." The dish *caril de galinha* is the fusion of Portuguese and Indian cuisine. It is a simple chicken curry from Goa, the long-lost home of the Portuguese in India. This dish is the Portuguese take on Indian chicken curry.

In a medium-sized bowl, coat the chicken with the curry powder and ¼ teaspoon of the salt for 30 minutes.

Set the SAUTÉ mode of the Instant Pot for 15 minutes.

Add the oil to the inner pot. Once the oil is hot, add the onion and fry for 3 to 4 minutes, or until lightly browned.

Add the ginger. Sauté for 30 to 40 seconds. Add the tomato paste, turmeric, red chili powder, the remaining salt and the cumin, and sauté for 40 to 50 seconds. Add the curry-coated chicken and let it brown, stirring frequently, about 5 minutes. Add the stock. Stir. Close the lid. Set the steam valve to the sealing position. Pressure cook at high pressure for 2 minutes. Wait for the natural release of steam.

Add the lemon juice and stir to mix. Next, add the coconut milk and cilantro. Simmer on SAUTÉ mode for 5 minutes.

Serve with rice.

9 oz (250 g) boneless chicken, cut into 1¼" to 1½" (3- to 4-cm) pieces

1 tsp curry powder

1¼ tsp (7 g) salt, divided

4 tbsp (60 ml) vegetable oil

1 cup (160 g) finely chopped yellow onion

1 tbsp (5 g) minced fresh ginger

1 tbsp (16 g) tomato paste or puree

½ tsp ground turmeric

1 tsp red chili powder

1 tsp ground cumin

2 tbsp (30 ml) plain chicken stock or water

1 tbsp (15 ml) fresh lemon juice

½ cup (120 ml) coconut milk

1 tbsp (1 g) chopped fresh cilantro

MEEN MOLLY

Coconut Milk and Fish Curry

Meen Molly is a beloved fish curry from Kerala. The dish was developed to suit the taste buds of Portuguese and British traders in the region. The folktale says that the curry got its name after the lady Molly, who curated it. Hence the name; *meen* means "fish." Along with the fish and coconut milk, this curry contains New World ingredients introduced by the Portuguese, such as sliced tomato and green chiles, making it more like a subtle stew.

4 tbsp (60 ml) coconut oil

1 tsp black mustard seeds

8 curry leaves

1 cup (160 g) sliced yellow onion

2 tbsp (10 g) julienned fresh ginger, divided

1 tbsp (10 g) sliced garlic

1 tsp ground turmeric

1 tsp red chili powder

2 cups (475 ml) coconut milk

1 tsp salt

9 oz (250 g) fish filet (seer, white pomfret, butterfish or king fish)

2 green chiles, such as jalapeños, Thai green chiles or serrano peppers, sliced

½ cup (90 g) seeded and sliced tomato

½ cup (120 ml) coconut cream or thick coconut milk

1 tbsp (1 g) chopped fresh cilantro, for garnish

Set the SAUTÉ mode of the Instant Pot for 30 minutes.

Add the oil to the inner pot. Once the oil is hot, add the mustard seeds and curry leaves. Once the seeds start to splutter, add the onion and fry for 3 to 4 minutes, or until the onion is lightly browned.

Add 1 tablespoon (5 g) of the ginger and the garlic, and sauté for 1 minute.

Add the turmeric and red chili powder, and sauté for 20 seconds.

Add the coconut milk and salt, and stir to combine. Once the curry starts to simmer, add the fish filet, green chiles and tomato, and cover the pot with the glass lid. Cook until the fish is tender.

Finally, add the thick coconut milk, gently stir and simmer the curry for 2 to 3 minutes.

Garnish with the cilantro and remaining julienned ginger. Serve with rice.

CHICKEN PATHIA

British-Style Chicken Curry with Mango Chutney

If you are a regular at Britain's curry houses, then chicken pathia curry might sound familiar. It is a typical takeaway-style sweet-and-sour chicken curry. The sweetness comes from the addition of white sugar, whereas delectable mango chutney is the secret ingredient responsible for making this curry unique. The flavors are enhanced while cooking in an Instant Pot, giving the curry a perfect taste and texture.

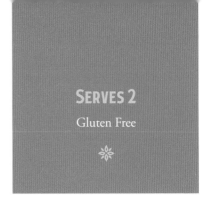

SERVES 2

Gluten Free

❋

Set the SAUTÉ mode of the Instant Pot for 15 minutes.

Add the oil to the inner pot. Once the oil is hot, add the onion and fry for 3 to 4 minutes, or until lightly browned. Add the ginger and garlic paste. Sauté for 30 to 40 seconds.

Add the tomato puree, tomato paste, red chili powder, curry powder and mango chutney, and sauté for 40 to 50 seconds. If the masala is sticking to the pot, add 1 to 2 tablespoons (15 to 30 ml) of stock.

Add the chicken pieces and bell pepper, and sauté for 5 minutes to sear. Add the ¼ cup (60 ml) of stock and salt. Stir to mix.

Close the lid. Set the steam valve to the sealing position. Pressure cook at high pressure for 4 minutes. Wait for the natural release of the steam.

Add the green chiles, lemon juice and cilantro. Mix nicely.

The chicken pathia is ready!

NOTE:

❋ You can use apple chutney or apricot chutney instead of mango chutney in this curry recipe.

4 tbsp (60 ml) vegetable oil

1 cup (160 g) finely chopped yellow onion

1 tbsp (20 g) ginger and garlic paste

¼ cup (63 g) tomato puree

2 tbsp (32 g) tomato paste

1 tsp red chili powder

2 tsp (4 g) curry powder

1 tbsp (16 g) mango chutney (see note)

¼ cup (60 ml) chicken stock or water, plus 1 to 2 tbsp (15 to 30 ml) if needed

9 oz (250 g) boneless chicken, cut into 1" to 1¼" (2.5- to 3-cm) pieces

1 cup (150 g) diced green bell pepper

1½ tsp (9 g) salt

2 mild green chiles, such as jalapeños, Thai green chiles or serrano peppers, sliced

1 tbsp (15 ml) fresh lemon juice

2 tbsp (2 g) chopped fresh cilantro

CHICKEN CHASHNI

Curry House–Style Sweet Chicken Curry

Another favorite from Britain's curry houses is chicken chashni. The word *chashni* in Hindi refers to a sugar syrup. In this curry, it describes the sweet taste of the dish. Before you get confused, let me tell you that no sugar syrup is added to this chicken curry. I find chicken chashni is a sweeter version of chicken tikka masala, but truly delicious and comforting.

4 tbsp (55 g) unsalted butter

1 tbsp (20 g) ginger and garlic paste

1 cup (250 g) tomato puree

¼ cup (60 g) tomato ketchup

1 tsp red chili powder

1 tsp curry powder

1 tsp ground cumin

9 oz (250 g) boneless chicken, cut into 1" (2.5-cm) pieces

¼ cup (60 ml) water or chicken stock

1¼ tsp (7 g) salt

¼ cup (60 ml) double cream

1 tsp dried fenugreek leaves (kasuri methi)

1 tbsp (3 g) chopped fresh mint leaves

1 tbsp (15 ml) fresh lemon juice

1 tbsp (1 g) chopped fresh cilantro, for garnish

2 tbsp (10 g) julienned fresh ginger, for garnish

Set the SAUTÉ mode of the Instant Pot for 10 minutes.

Add the butter to the inner pot. Once the butter is hot, add the ginger and garlic paste. Sauté for 20 to 30 seconds. Add the tomato puree, tomato ketchup, red chili powder, curry powder and cumin, and sauté for 2 to 3 minutes.

Add the chicken. Sauté for 5 minutes, or until it turns almost opaque.

Add the water and salt, and stir to mix. Close the lid. Set the steam valve to the sealing position. Pressure cook at high pressure for 2 minutes. Wait for the natural release of steam.

Set the SAUTÉ mode for 5 minutes. Add the cream, fenugreek leaves, mint leaves and lemon juice, and stir to mix. Simmer the curry for 5 minutes, stirring at regular intervals.

Garnish with the cilantro and ginger.

LEFTOVER TURKEY CURRY

Curry with Shredded Turkey

SERVES 2

Gluten Free

❁

Leftover shredded turkey combined in a silky smooth curry sauce is what this dish is all about. After Thanksgiving or party dinners, if you have extra roasted turkey, then this is the ideal way to use it. You can add bite-sized pieces of turkey or shred it and add them to the curry. Serve it with rice or flatbread.

Gently crush the nigella, fennel, cumin and coriander seeds to a coarse powder, using a mortar and pestle or spice grinder. Set aside.

Set the SAUTÉ mode of the Instant Pot for 30 minutes.

Add the oil to the inner pot. Once the oil is hot, add the crushed seeds and red onion. Sauté for 3 to 4 minutes, or until the onion becomes lightly browned. Add the ginger and garlic paste. Sauté for 30 to 40 seconds.

Add the crushed tomato, tomato paste, turmeric, red chili powder and salt. Sauté for 2 to 3 minutes.

Next, add the shredded turkey, coconut milk, bell pepper, green chiles and garam masala. Stir to mix.

Cover the pot with the glass lid. Simmer in SAUTÉ mode for 5 minutes, stirring at regular intervals to avoid burning the curry.

Garnish with the cilantro and serve.

1 tsp nigella seeds

1 tsp fennel seeds

1 tsp cumin seeds

1 tsp coriander seeds

4 tbsp (60 ml) vegetable oil

1 cup (160 g) finely chopped red onion

1 tbsp (20 g) ginger and garlic paste

1 cup (244 g) canned crushed tomato

1 tbsp (16 g) tomato paste

1 tsp ground turmeric

1 tsp red chili powder

1 tsp salt

9 oz (250 g) leftover roasted turkey, shredded

1 cup (240 ml) coconut milk

1 cup (150 g) seeded and diced red bell pepper

2 mild green chiles, such as jalapeños, Thai green chiles or serrano peppers, sliced

1 tsp garam masala

1 tbsp (1 g) chopped fresh cilantro, for garnish

CHICKEN XACUTI

Spicy Chicken Curry from Goa

Xacuti is a famous Goan masala paste that is used to make a variety of curries with vegetables, meat and seafood. This is a typical Goa-style chicken curry with a hint of various spices, such as cardamom, cloves and coriander, combined with the creaminess of coconut milk. Chicken xacuti is one of my favorite curries to make in an Instant Pot because the flavors of the masala penetrate the layers of chicken, making it perfectly juicy and full of flavor.

1 tbsp (5 g) coriander seeds

1 tsp cumin seeds

1 tsp white poppy seeds

1 tsp fennel seeds

1 tsp black peppercorns

4 dried Kashmiri red chiles

1 star anise

1 black cardamom pod

2 green cardamom pods

4 whole cloves

¼ whole nutmeg

½ cup (42 g) grated coconut

¼ cup (55 g) coconut oil, divided

1 cup (160 g) chopped yellow onion, divided

1 tbsp (5 g) chopped fresh ginger

1 tbsp (10 g) chopped garlic

1 cup (240 ml) water, divided

½ cup (90 g) chopped tomato

1¼ tsp (7 g) salt

½ tsp red chili powder

1 tsp ground turmeric

9 oz (250 g) bone-in chicken, cut into 1¼" to 1½" (3- to 4-cm) bone-in pieces

Set the SAUTÉ mode of the Instant Pot for 10 minutes.

Add the coriander, cumin, poppy, and fennel seeds, black peppercorns, red chiles, star anise, cardamom pods, cloves and nutmeg. Dry roast for 1 minute. Transfer to a plate.

Next, dry roast the coconut for 30 to 40 seconds (see notes). Transfer to the same plate as the spices.

Add 2 tablespoons (28 g) of the coconut oil to the inner pot. Once the oil is hot, add ½ cup (80 g) of the onion.

Fry the onion for 3 to 4 minutes, or until lightly golden. Add the ginger and garlic. Sauté for 1 minute.

Now, leaving the oil in the inner pot and transferring the fried mixture to a blender, make a smooth paste of the fried onion, dry-roasted spices and coconut, using ¼ cup (60 ml) of the water. Set aside.

Set the SAUTÉ mode for 10 minutes. Add the remaining 2 tablespoons (27 g) of oil. Fry the remaining ½ cup (80 g) of onion for 3 to 4 minutes, or until lightly golden. Add the tomato, salt, red chili powder and turmeric, and fry for 2 to 3 minutes.

Next, add the blended curry paste and chicken, and sauté the pieces for 3 minutes, or until they become almost opaque and start to release liquid.

Add the remaining ¾ cup (180 ml) of water. Stir. Close the lid. Set the steam valve to the sealing position. Pressure cook at high pressure for 4 minutes. Wait for the natural release of steam.

Serve with rice.

NOTES:

✻ Do not dry roast the coconut with the other spices, as it might burn and taste bitter. It is safer to roast it separately.

✻ Four minutes of cook time will give you fall-off-the-bone, well-done chicken, whereas 2 minutes will give you medium-cooked chicken.

ONE-POT CURRY MEALS

We all need time-saving, comforting, minimal-cleanup and maximum-flavor one-pot meal recipes in our life. In Indian cuisine, you will find plenty of one-pot meals. The list is quite exhaustive, from a variety of porridges to rice dishes and stews. From the Mughal emperors Jahangir to Aurangzeb, and later the British, all fell in love with Indian rice and lentil one-pot porridge *khichdi*, the inspiration behind kedgeree. And then, such one-pot dishes as *konji* (congee) traveled across the geographic boundaries. Today, each Southeast Asian country has its version of congee. In South Africa, Bunny Chow (page 214) is the perfect example of creative, curried one-pot meals that can comfort every taste bud.

The one-pot curry meals in this chapter are my personal favorites as a busy home-maker. They are wholesome, nourishing, customizable and, most important, delicious to the core. Plus, I don't have to juggle different stove burners and utensils to create a single meal. Such dishes as Misal Pav (page 218) or Bengali Matar Ghugni (page 221) need a buttered toast on the side to soak up all the extra sauce and to provide carbohydrates to balance the protein from the legumes. On the other hand, with my Lehsuni Palak Khichdi (page 222), you do not need any side dishes at all. It is a perfect, vegetarian, one-pot family meal.

In my mother's kitchen, all of these one-pot meals were cooked in a conventional stovetop pressure cooker. But for me, the Instant Pot has been a total game changer. The cooking time has been reduced to almost half, and with such modes as PORRIDGE, SOUP or PRESSURE COOK, it is convenient to pick a custom cooking mode for each dish to get the flawless texture. Once you try these one-pot Indian curries in an Instant Pot, they will become regulars in your everyday meal menu.

Dal Dhokli

Pigeon Peas Curry with Handmade Wheat Pasta

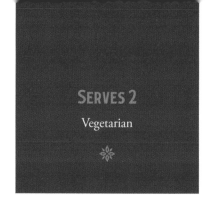

SERVES 2

Vegetarian

If you are a vegetarian and looking for a fulfilling one-pot Indian meal, then my top answer is: *dal dhokli*. This is among those Indian recipes that I feel are perfect for the Instant Pot. It is a simple Gujarati dish of yellow pigeon peas and handmade wheat pasta (*dhokli*) simmered in it. Pressure cook the dal in an Instant Pot and then cook the homemade wheat pasta squares in the curry. Honestly, it's super delicious and wholesome.

Rinse the pigeon peas until the water runs clear. Soak in water for 15 minutes.

Set the SAUTÉ mode of the Instant Pot for 8 minutes.

Add the ghee to the inner pot. Once the ghee is hot, add the cumin and mustard seeds, asafetida, ginger and curry leaves. Sauté for 40 to 50 seconds.

Add the tomato, salt, red chili powder and turmeric, and sauté until the tomato is mashed up or softened, 2 to 3 minutes. Add the tamarind paste and brown sugar, and stir to mix.

Drain all the water from the soaked pigeon peas. Add them to the inner pot. Stir to combine.

Add the fresh water and stir. Close the lid. Set the steam valve to the sealing position. Pressure cook at high pressure for 8 minutes. Wait for the natural release of steam.

Meanwhile, prepare the wheat pasta: In a medium-sized bowl, combine the flour, salt, turmeric, red chili powder, carom seeds and ghee. Mix nicely. Using very little water at a time, form a smooth, soft, nonsticky dough. Cover with a clean muslin cloth or cheesecloth and set aside.

Set the SAUTÉ mode of the Instant Pot for 12 minutes. Let the dal simmer.

Form the dough into four equal-sized balls. Sprinkling a clean surface with whole wheat flour, roll out each dough ball to a thin 10- to 12-inch (25- to 30-cm) square. Using a knife or a pizza cutter, cut each disk into 1-inch (2.5-cm) squares. Arrange them on a baking sheet. Repeat with the remaining dough.

Add the wheat pasta to the dal and stir to mix. Cover the pot with the glass lid. Cook the pasta until the timer beeps, gently stirring halfway through the cook time without breaking the pasta.

Garnish with the cilantro and red onion to serve.

1 cup (170 g) dried split pigeon peas (toor dal)

2 tbsp (28 g) ghee

1 tsp cumin seeds

1 tsp black mustard seeds

¼ tsp asafetida

1 tbsp (5 g) grated fresh ginger

8 curry leaves

½ cup (90 g) chopped tomato

2 tsp (12 g) salt

1 tsp red chili powder

1 tsp ground turmeric

1 tbsp (15 g) tamarind paste

1 tbsp (15 g) light brown sugar or jaggery powder

3 cups (720 ml) water

2 tbsp (2 g) chopped fresh cilantro, for garnish

2 tbsp (20 g) chopped red onion, for garnish

Wheat Pasta (Dhokli)

1 cup (130 g) whole wheat flour, plus more for dusting

½ tsp salt

½ tsp ground turmeric

½ tsp red chili powder

½ tsp carom seeds (ajwain)

1 tbsp (14 g) ghee

¼ to ½ cup (30 to 60 ml) water

KONJI

Indian-Style Rice Porridge

From broken hearts and runny noses to gloomy days, Mom's congee has been a big savior for most of us. Congee is a nourishing Asian-style savory porridge served with a variety of toppings. The idea of interesting toppings makes me excited about eating the dish. This is my version of Indian konji, which is delicious and comforting to the core.

4 tbsp (50 g) dried yellow moong beans

1 cup (200 g) uncooked short-grain white rice (see note)

4 tbsp (60 ml) sesame oil

1 tbsp (10 g) sliced garlic

1 cup (160 g) sliced yellow onion

1 (1" [2.5-cm])-long piece cinnamon stick

4 whole cloves

¼ cup (38 g) diced carrot

¼ cup (35 g) peeled, seeded and diced winter squash

6 cups (1.4 L) water

2 tsp (12 g) salt

¼ tsp ground turmeric

1 cup (30 g) baby spinach leaves

2 tbsp (2 g) chopped fresh cilantro, for garnish

2 tbsp (30 ml) mustard oil, for drizzling

In the Instant Pot set to SAUTÉ mode, dry roast the moong beans in for 2 minutes to release a nutty aroma. Transfer to a bowl and add the rice to the bowl.

Rinse the moong beans and rice until the water runs clear. Soak in water for 15 minutes.

Set the SAUTÉ mode of the Instant Pot for 12 minutes.

Add the oil to the inner pot. Once the oil is hot, add the garlic and fry until lightly golden, 3 to 4 minutes. Transfer to a bowl. Repeat the process with the onion. Transfer to the same bowl as the garlic. Set aside.

To the same oil, add the cinnamon stick and cloves, and sauté for 20 seconds.

Drain all the water from soaked rice and moong beans. Add to the spices in the inner pot along with carrot and squash. Sauté for 1 minute. Add the water, salt and turmeric, and mix.

Close the lid. Set the steam valve to the sealing position. Cook in PORRIDGE mode for 10 minutes. Wait for the steam to release.

Add the spinach leaves and stir to mix into the hot konji.

Serve the konji in a bowl topped with the fried garlic and onion, cilantro, plus a drizzle of mustard oil.

NOTE:

❋ **A starchy short-grain rice works best for making konji.**

HALEEM

Broken Wheat, Meat, Legumes and Vegetables Casserole

Haleem is a widely popular stew from the Indian subcontinent, Central Asia and the Middle East. Its origin is traced to the historic Arabian dish called *harees*. The dish is mainly consumed during the holy month of Ramadan. It is a super healthy, fulfilling one-pot meal made with broken wheat, meat, legumes, ghee, vegetables and spices. The slow cooking of seven to eight hours over the wood fire is the secret behind the famous haleem from Hyderabad, the city of royals. I am sure my Instant Pot version of this classic stew will perform the same comforting, toothsome magic for you as it does for me.

SERVES 2

Combine the broken wheat, pink lentils, moong beans, chickpeas and rice in a bowl. Rinse until the water runs clear. Soak in water for 30 minutes.

Clean and pat dry the meat pieces. Set aside.

Set the SAUTÉ mode of the Instant Pot for 30 minutes.

Add the oil to the inner pot. Once the oil is hot, add the meat pieces. Sauté them until browned on all sides, 5 to 6 minutes. Transfer to a plate.

Add the cardamom pods, cloves, bay leaf and black peppercorns to the inner pot. Sauté for 20 seconds. Add the red onion and fry until golden brown, 4 to 5 minutes.

Make a coarse paste of the green chiles, ginger and garlic in a mortar and pestle or blender. Add to the inner pot. Sauté for 1 minute. Return the meat pieces to the pot along with the water, salt and garam masala, and stir to mix.

(continued)

1 cup (145 g) broken wheat (dalia)

¼ cup (45 g) dried pink lentils (masoor dal)

¼ cup (50 g) dried yellow moong beans

2 tbsp (25 g) dried split chickpeas (chana dal)

¼ cup (50 g) uncooked short-grain white rice

9 oz (250 g) boneless lamb or goat meat, cut into 1" to 1¼" (2.5- to 3-cm) pieces (see note)

½ cup (120 ml) vegetable oil

4 green cardamom pods

4 whole cloves

1 bay leaf

1 tsp black peppercorns, crushed

1 cup (160 g) sliced red onion

2 mild green chiles, such as jalapeños, Thai green chiles or serrano peppers, chopped

1 (1" [2.5-cm]) piece fresh ginger, roughly sliced

5 cloves garlic

3 cups (720 ml) water

2 tsp (12 g) salt

1 tsp garam masala

Drain all the water from the soaked wheat and legumes. Add them to the inner pot along with the ghee. Stir to mix nicely. Set the Instant Pot to SLOW COOK for 4 hours on low. The consistency of haleem is like a thick, melt-in-your-mouth porridge. Remove and discard the bay leaf before serving.

Garnish with the fried onions, julienned ginger, cilantro and mint leaves, and drizzle with the lime juice.

NOTE:

✳ **For extra flavor, you can make haleem with bone-in meat pieces. Later, after cooking, debone the meat, chop or shred it and add back to the porridge.**

1 tbsp (14 g) ghee

2 tbsp (50 g) fried onions (brista), for garnish

2 tbsp (10 g) julienned ginger, for garnish

2 tbsp (2 g) chopped fresh cilantro, for garnish

2 tbsp (3 g) chopped fresh mint leaves, for garnish

Juice of 1 lime, for garnish

BISI BELLE BATH

One-Pot Vegetable, Rice and Legumes Casserole

A traditional curried meal from Karnataka, *bisi belle bath* literally translates into "hot legumes rice dish." The Instant Pot's PRESSURE COOK mode is a real blessing to make this one-pot casserole. Tone down the spices and chiles by reducing the quantity or by adding more coconut to the masala paste. The soul of a good bisi belle bath is the masala paste made from scratch, as I suggest in the recipe. No curry powder will give you that satisfying taste.

1 tbsp (13 g) dried split chickpeas (chana dal)

1 cup (170 g) dried split pigeon peas (toor dal)

½ cup (100 g) short-grain white rice

4 tsp (7 g) coriander seeds

1 tsp cumin seeds

2 whole cloves

½ tsp black peppercorns

2 dried red chiles

2 cloves garlic, chopped

2 tbsp (10 g) grated coconut

1 tbsp (15 g) tamarind paste

1 tbsp (15 ml) peanut oil

2 to 4 tbsp (30 to 60 ml) hot water, for blending

4 tbsp (55 g) ghee, plus 1 tbsp (14 g), for serving

1½ tsp (6 g) black mustard seeds (rai)

¼ cup (36 g) peanuts

¼ tsp asafetida

6 to 8 curry leaves

2 dried red chiles, such as Kashmiri

½ cup (80 g) chopped shallots or onion

Rinse the chickpeas and pigeon peas until the water runs clear, and soak them in water for 10 minutes. Similarly, soak the rice in a separate bowl.

In the Instant Pot set to SAUTÉ mode, dry roast the coriander seeds, cumin seeds, cloves, black peppercorns, red chiles, garlic and coconut for 40 to 50 seconds. In a blender, blend into a paste along with the tamarind paste, peanut oil and 2 to 4 tablespoons (30 to 60 ml) of hot water. Set this masala paste aside.

Set the SAUTÉ mode of the Instant Pot for 8 minutes.

Add the 4 tablespoons (55 g) of ghee to the inner pot. Once the ghee is hot, add the mustard seeds, peanuts, asafetida, curry leaves, red chiles and shallots. Sauté for 2 minutes, or until shallots turn translucent.

(continued)

½ cup (90 g) chopped tomato

¼ cup (33 g) peeled and diced carrot

¼ cup (25 g) chopped green beans

⅓ cup (45 g) peeled and diced bottle gourd (calabash)

6 to 8 pieces drumstick, cleaned and peeled (see note)

1 tsp ground turmeric

½ tsp red chili powder

2 tsp (12 g) salt

3 cups (720 ml) water

2 tbsp (30 g) dark brown sugar or jaggery powder

Next, drain all the water from the soaked legumes. Add them to the inner pot. Sauté for 1 minute. Add the tomato, carrot, green beans, bottle gourd, drumstick, turmeric, red chili powder and salt, and sauté until the timer beeps.

Add the water and stir. Close the lid. Set the steam valve to the sealing position. Pressure cook at high pressure for 10 minutes. Wait for the natural release of the steam.

Drain all the water from the soaked rice. Add the rice to the inner pot along with the prepared masala paste and brown sugar, and stir to mix. Close the lid. Set the steam valve to the sealing position. Pressure cook at high pressure for 5 minutes.

Drizzle with the tablespoon (14 g) of ghee and serve.

NOTE:

❉ **Drumstick is the stem of a moringa plant. It is a vegetable commonly found in Asia and has nothing to do with chicken drumsticks.**

BUNNY CHOW

One-Pot Meat, Chickpea and Potato Stew

When it comes to Bunny Chow, I am always caught up in a debate whether it is a sandwich or a curried meal. A delicious curried street food from South Africa, with no actual bunnies in it, Bunny Chow got its name from the Bania community of traders who started settling in South Africa and selling this one-pot stew in hollow bread bowls. It has meat, beans, vegetables, spices and everything delicious, which makes it one of the most soul-satisfying kinds of street food.

SERVES 2

Gluten Free

Set the SAUTÉ mode of the Instant Pot for 8 minutes.

Add the oil to the inner pot. Once the oil is hot, add the ginger and garlic, and sauté for 40 to 50 seconds. Add the red onion and fry for 3 to 4 minutes, or until lightly browned.

Next, add the canned tomato, tomato paste, paprika, curry powder, cumin and salt. Sauté for 2 minutes. Add the chicken breast and sear until it becomes almost opaque, 2 minutes per side.

Add the water. Close the lid. Set the steam valve to the sealing position. Pressure cook at high pressure for 5 minutes. Manually release the steam.

Remove the cooked chicken from the broth, using tongs, and shred it. Add it back to the curry along with the chickpeas and potato. Stir to mix. Close the lid. Set the steam valve to the sealing position. Pressure cook for 2 minutes. Wait for the natural release of steam.

Garnish with the cilantro. To serve, hollow out a round bread or slice a hot dog bun or *pav*. Fill it with the curry and the Bunny Chow is ready!

4 tbsp (60 ml) vegetable oil

1 tbsp (5 g) finely minced fresh ginger

1 tbsp (10 g) finely minced garlic

½ cup (80 g) finely chopped red onion

1 cup (244 g) canned crushed tomato

2 tbsp (32 g) tomato paste

1 tsp paprika or red chili powder

1 tsp curry powder

1 tsp ground cumin

1¼ tsp (7 g) salt

9 oz (250 g) chicken breast

1½ cups (360 ml) water or chicken stock

1 cup (240 g) canned chickpeas, drained and rinsed

1 cup (170 g) finely chopped potato

2 tbsp (2 g) chopped fresh cilantro, for garnish

MULLIGATAWNY

Anglo Indian Curried Soup

One of my favorite one-pot curry meals is the classic mulligatawny—a popular Anglo Indian stew. Mulligatawny has its roots in Madras. *Milagu* means "pepper" and *tanni* means "water," and that is how the soup got its name: peppery water. This spicy lentil soup became widely popular among the British residents during their stay in South India. I make it more fulfilling by combining a variety of vegetables, lentils, rice and a dash of coconut milk. In an Instant Pot, it takes less than 20 minutes to stir up a delicious bowl of mulligatawny.

½ cup (90 g) dried pink lentils (masoor dal)

¼ cup (49 g) uncooked white rice

4 tbsp (60 ml) vegetable oil

1 bay leaf

1 tbsp (5 g) finely chopped fresh ginger

1 tbsp (10 g) finely chopped garlic

1 tbsp (8 g) finely chopped celery

½ cup (80 g) chopped yellow onion

½ cup (55 g) finely chopped carrot

¼ cup (32 g) cored, peeled, and finely chopped apple

3 cups (710 ml) vegetable stock

1 tsp curry powder

1 tsp freshly ground black pepper

1¼ tsp (7 g) salt

1 cup (240 ml) coconut milk

1 tbsp (15 ml) fresh lemon juice

2 tbsp (2 g) finely chopped fresh cilantro

Rinse the lentils and rice until the water runs clear. Soak in water for 15 minutes.

Set the SAUTÉ mode of the Instant Pot for 5 minutes.

Add the oil to the inner pot. Once the oil is hot, add the bay leaf, ginger, garlic, celery and onion. Sauté for 2 minutes, or until the onion becomes translucent.

Drain all the water from the soaked lentils and rice. Add them to the inner pot along with the carrot and apple. Sauté for 30 to 40 seconds.

Add the stock, curry powder, pepper and salt, and stir to mix. Close the lid. Set the steam valve to the sealing position. Cook in STEW mode for 10 minutes. Release the steam manually. Blend the stew, using an immersion blender. Alternatively, you can serve mulligatawny without blending it.

Add the coconut milk, lemon juice and cilantro, and stir to mix. Simmer for 5 minutes in SAUTÉ mode. Remove and discard the bay leaf before serving.

Serve warm.

MISAL PAV

Spicy Sprouted Moth Bean Curry

Misal is a spicy moth bean sprouted curry served with buttered pav bread. It is one of the most popular street foods of Mumbai (formerly known as Bombay). The Portuguese introduced the bread-eating culture in Goa and from there the bread traveled to Bombay and other coastal areas. Today, apart from misal, there are many other Indian dishes enjoyed with pav bread on the side. The soft, pillowy, texture of the pav perfectly absorbs the flavorsome curry of the misal. If you are not comfortable with red chiles, then reduce the quantity in the masala paste and curry to almost one-fourth, because misal is a highly spicy curry.

SERVES 2

Vegan, Gluten Free

Clean and rinse the moth bean sprouts. Set aside.

In the Instant Pot set to SAUTÉ mode, dry roast the coriander seeds, garlic and dried red chiles for 1 minute. Transfer to a blender. Similarly, dry roast the coconut for 40 to 50 seconds. Add it to the same blender as the spices. Blend into a smooth paste, using the 4 tablespoons (60 ml) of hot water. Set aside.

Set the SAUTÉ mode of the Instant Pot for 10 minutes.

Add the oil to the inner pot. Once the oil is hot, add the mustard seeds and curry leaves. Once the seeds start to splutter, add the red onion and fry for 2 to 3 minutes, or until lightly golden.

Add the ginger and garlic paste. Sauté for 40 to 50 seconds. Add the tomato, salt, turmeric and red chili powder. Sauté for 2 minutes.

Next, add the drained moth bean sprouts, prepared spiced coconut paste, water, and stir to mix. Close the lid. Set the steam valve to the sealing position. Pressure cook at high pressure for 10 minutes. Wait for the natural release of steam.

Add the brown sugar, garam masala, lemon juice and cilantro. Stir to mix.

Serve topped with sev (a store-bought gram flour snack), additional chopped onion and cilantro, with a side of pav bread.

NOTES:

❋ Misal is a medium to highly spicy curry. Adjust the number of red chiles according to personal preference.

❋ You can make misal with green moong bean sprouts as well.

1½ cups (150 g) moth bean sprouts

1 tbsp (5 g) coriander seeds

6 cloves garlic

4 dried Kashmiri red chiles (see note)

¼ cup (21 g) grated coconut

4 tbsp (60 ml) hot water

4 tbsp (60 ml) peanut oil

1 tsp black mustard seeds

6 to 8 curry leaves

1 cup (160 g) finely chopped red onion, plus more for serving

1 tbsp (20 g) ginger and garlic paste

¼ cup (45 g) canned tomato

1 tsp salt

1 tsp ground turmeric

½ tsp Kashmiri red chili powder

3 cups (720 ml) water

1 tbsp (15 g) light brown sugar or jaggery powder

½ tsp garam masala

2 tbsp (30 ml) fresh lemon juice

2 tbsp (2 g) finely chopped fresh cilantro, plus more for serving

BENGALI MATAR GHUGNI

Dried White Peas Stew

This *ghugni* is a flavorsome, sweet, sour, spicy, savory stew of dried white peas and potatoes. Everything is cooked together to create a hearty bowl of goodness. The dish has its origin in Kolkatta (previously called Calcutta). It is a widely popular street food and breakfast dish in Bengal. Ghugni is one of the best one-pot curried meals that requires only toasted bread slices on the side to soak up all the flavors of the stew.

1 cup (180 g) dried white peas (matar)

2 green chiles, such as jalapeños, Thai green chiles or serrano peppers, chopped

4 cloves garlic

4 tbsp (60 ml) mustard oil

1 bay leaf

4 green cardamom pods

4 whole cloves

1 (1" [2.5-cm])-long piece cinnamon stick

2 dried red chiles

1 tbsp (5 g) sliced coconut

½ cup (80 g) finely chopped red onion

1 tbsp (20 g) ginger and garlic paste

⅓ cup (60 g) chopped tomato

2 tsp (12 g) salt

1 tsp ground turmeric

1 tsp red chili powder

1 tsp ground cumin

1 cup (170 g) diced potato

1 tbsp (14 g) ghee

1½ cups (360 ml) water

½ tsp garam masala

1 tbsp (15 g) light brown sugar or jaggery powder

2 tbsp (30 ml) fresh lemon juice

2 tbsp (2 g) chopped fresh cilantro

Rinse the dried peas until the water runs clear. Soak in water for 5 hours or overnight.

Crush the green chiles and garlic to a coarse paste, using a mortar and pestle or blender.

Set the SAUTÉ mode of the Instant Pot for 15 minutes.

Add the oil to the inner pot. Once the oil is smoking hot, add the bay leaf, cardamom pods, cloves, cinnamon stick, red chiles and coconut. Fry for 40 to 50 seconds.

Add the red onion and fry until lightly golden. Add the ginger and garlic paste. Sauté for 30 to 40 seconds.

Add the tomato, salt, turmeric, red chili powder and cumin, and sauté for 2 minutes, or until the tomato breaks down completely.

Drain all the water from the soaked peas. Add them to the inner pot along with the potato, ghee, prepared green chile paste, water, garam masala and brown sugar. Stir to mix.

Close the lid. Set the steam valve to the sealing position. Pressure cook at high pressure for 10 minutes. Wait for the natural release of the steam. Add the lemon juice and cilantro. Remove and discard the bay leaf before serving.

Serve with toasted bread.

LEHSUNI PALAK KHICHDI

Garlicky Rice, Yellow Moong Bean and Spinach Porridge

Khichdi is a popular casserole from the Indian subcontinent. A combination of lentils and vegetables are cooked with rice in one pot to create a wholesome and delicious vegetarian dish. From the food memoirs of Mughal emperors to the British kedgeree, one can find a lot of interesting tales about the khichdi. This recipe is for a spinach and garlic–flavored moong bean and rice khichdi that is a comforting bowl of green goodness. If you are a garlic lover like me, then this khichdi will soon become your favorite curried meal.

SERVES 2

Vegetarian, Gluten Free

Combine the rice and moong beans. Rinse until the water runs clear. Soak in water for 15 minutes.

Bring 2 cups (480 ml) of water to a boil in the Instant Pot. Add the spinach leaves. Cook for 1 minute. Transfer the leaves to a blender along with the green chile, ginger and garlic cloves. Blend into a smooth paste. Set aside. Discard the water from the Instant Pot.

Set the SAUTÉ mode of the Instant Pot for 10 minutes.

Add the ghee to the inner pot. Once the ghee is hot, add the dried red chiles, sliced garlic, asafetida and cumin seeds, and fry for 50 seconds. Add the red onion and fry until lightly golden.

Drain all the water from the soaked rice and moong beans. Add to the pot. Sauté until the timer goes off. Add the remaining 2¼ cups (540 ml) of water, salt and red chili powder, and mix. Close the lid. Set the steam valve to the sealing position. Pressure cook at high pressure for 6 minutes. Wait for the natural release of steam.

Add the spinach puree to the khichdi. Stir to combine. Cover the pot with the glass lid and let it rest for 5 minutes. Serve the khichdi warm.

1 cup (200 g) uncooked short-grain white rice

⅓ cup (67 g) dried yellow moong beans

4¼ cups (1 L) water, divided

2 cups (60 g) spinach leaves

1 green chile, such as jalapeño, Thai green chile or serrano pepper, chopped

1 tbsp (5 g) chopped fresh ginger

2 cloves garlic

4 tbsp (55 g) ghee

2 dried red chiles

1 tbsp (10 g) sliced garlic

¼ tsp asafetida

1 tsp cumin seeds

½ cup (80 g) finely chopped red onion

1 tsp salt

½ tsp red chili powder

ANDA DAL

Eggs Poached in a Lentil Curry

This *anda dal* recipe comes from my husband's Sikh family. After the partition of India and Pakistan, his family settled in a small town in the foothills of Himalaya. Over the decades, many family recipes got lost with time, but one recipe of eggs cooked in a dal remained consistent. This is the kind of dish you will not so easily find in a restaurant or cookbook. You can easily make this comforting egg lentil curry, a delicacy for busy weeknights or cold winter nights, in an Instant Pot in under 30 minutes.

1 cup (200 g) dried pink lentils (masoor dal)

2 tbsp (30 ml) cooking oil

1 tsp cumin seeds

1 tbsp (10 g) finely chopped garlic

½ cup (80 g) finely chopped red onion

½ cup (90 g) finely chopped tomato

1 green chile, such as jalapeño, Thai green chile or serrano pepper, chopped

1 tsp ground turmeric

1 tsp red chili powder

1 tsp salt

1¼ cups (300 ml) water

4 large eggs (see note)

2 tbsp (2 g) chopped fresh cilantro leaves, for garnish

Rinse the lentils with water until it runs clear. Soak in water for 15 minutes.

Set the SAUTÉ mode of the Instant Pot for 8 minutes.

Add the oil to the inner pot. Once the oil is hot, add the cumin seeds and garlic, and sauté for 40 to 50 seconds. Add the red onion, and fry until lightly browned, 3 to 4 minutes.

Add the tomato, green chile, turmeric, red chili powder and salt, and sauté for 2 minutes, or until the tomato turns soft.

Drain all the water from the soaked lentils. Add them to the inner pot. Sauté until the timer beeps. Add the 1¼ cups (300 ml) of water, and stir to mix.

Close the lid. Set the steam valve to the sealing position. Pressure cook at high pressure for 5 minutes. Wait for the natural release of steam.

Set the SAUTÉ mode for 5 minutes. Make four small dents in the curry. Break and add one egg to each dent. Cover the Instant Pot with a glass lid. Simmer the curry for 5 minutes, or until eggs are perfectly set.

Garnish with the cilantro and serve.

NOTE

❊ There are two ways of making this dal. You can add whisked eggs or you can directly break the whole egg into the dal and poach for a few minutes like a shakshuka. I am following a shakshuka style in this recipe.

OATS KHICHDI

Yellow Moong Bean and Whole Oats Savory Porridge

Oats khichdi is an Indian-style porridge packed with vegetables and yellow moong beans, a fabulous vegetarian one-pot meal that comes together effortlessly under 20 minutes in an Instant Pot. It is a wholesome recipe that replaces rice with oats, has lots of veggies for nutrition and moong dal for protein.

SERVES 2

Vegetarian, Gluten Free

Rinse the moong beans until the water runs clear. Soak in water for 10 minutes.

Set the SAUTÉ mode of the Instant Pot for 8 minutes.

Add the ghee to the inner pot. Once the ghee is hot, add the cumin seeds, asafetida and ginger, and sauté for 40 to 50 seconds. Add the red onion and fry until it is lightly golden, 3 to 4 minutes.

Add the tomato, red chili powder, turmeric and salt, and sauté for 2 minutes, or until the tomato breaks down completely.

Drain all the water from the soaked moong beans. Add them to the pot along with the oats, peas and carrot. Sauté until the timer beeps.

Add the water and stir to combine. Close the lid. Set the steam valve to the sealing position. Pressure cook at high pressure for 6 minutes. Wait for the natural release of steam.

Add the spinach and stir to mix. Cover with the glass lid for 2 minutes.

Serve warm with dahi (curd) and chutney.

½ cup (100 g) dried yellow moong beans

4 tbsp (55 g) ghee

1 tsp cumin seeds

¼ tsp asafetida

1 tbsp (5 g) grated fresh ginger

1 cup (160 g) finely chopped red onion

½ cup (90 g) finely chopped tomato

1 tsp red chili powder

1 tsp ground turmeric

2 tsp (12 g) salt

1 cup (80 g) whole oats

½ cup (75 g) green peas

½ cup (65 g) diced carrot

3 cups (720 ml) water

1 cup (30 g) spinach leaves

QUINOA PONGAL

One-Pot Quinoa and Yellow Moong Bean Casserole

Pongal is a classic porridge from South India. This savory, vegetarian recipe is inspired by the forever favorite *ven pongal*—a simple, one-pot meal of yellow moong dal and rice with a delicious tempering of ghee, cashews and curry leaves on top. In this pongal recipe, rice is replaced with more nutritious quinoa. And it tastes equally delicious! Serve this Indian-style quinoa porridge with green chutney or coconut chutney to spice up the flavor.

½ cup dried yellow moong beans

4 tbsp (55 g) ghee

1 tsp black mustard seeds

2 tsp (4 g) cumin seeds

¼ tsp asafetida

1 tsp (4 g) skinned black gram (urad dal)

10 curry leaves

1 tbsp (5 g) grated fresh ginger

2 tbsp (18 g) roughly chopped cashews

1 green chile, such as jalapeño, Thai green chile or serrano pepper, chopped

½ cup (87 g) uncooked quinoa or (100 g) uncooked short-grain rice, rinsed well

1¼ tsp (7 g) salt

2 cups (480 ml) water

2 tsp (3 g) crushed black peppercorns

1 tbsp (1 g) chopped fresh cilantro

In the Instant Pot set to SAUTÉ mode, dry roast the moong beans for 1 minute. Transfer to a bowl. Rinse until the water runs clear. Soak in water for 10 minutes.

Meanwhile, set the SAUTÉ mode of the Instant Pot for 12 minutes and add the ghee to the inner pot. Once the ghee is hot, add the mustard seeds, cumin seeds, asafetida, black gram, curry leaves, ginger, cashews and green chile. Sauté for 1 minute.

Add the rinsed quinoa to the pot. Sauté for 1 minute.

Drain all the water from the moong beans. Add them to the pot along with the salt and fresh 2 cups (480 ml) of water. Stir to mix.

Close the lid. Set the steam valve to the sealing position. Pressure cook at high pressure for 6 minutes. Wait for the natural release of the steam.

Add the black peppercorns and cilantro. Mix nicely.

Serve with coconut chutney.

INDIAN KITCHEN STAPLES

I always take great care to ensure that my recipes work for every person who tries them out for the first time. To help you navigate this book like a pro, I am sharing tried-and-true tips about the basic spices used throughout this cookbook, cooking oils and a few standard recipe-related pointers.

Essential Spice Powders: Red chili powder, ground turmeric and ground coriander are the three basic spices you need for almost all recipes in this cookbook.

Garam Masala: This is an Indian spice blend made with a variety of whole spices. Do not confuse garam masala with curry powder. Both have different tastes and flavor profiles. A garam masala is always added toward the end of the dish for aroma and taste.

Whole Spices: Throughout the book, I have used a variety of whole spices to flavor the curries. Some essential ones are cumin seeds, black and yellow mustard seeds, fenugreek seeds, fennel seeds, bay leaf, green and black cardamom pods, whole cloves and cinnamon sticks. You can store all of these for a year in airtight containers at room temperature.

Dried Fenugreek Leaves: Dried fenugreek leaves are known as *kasuri methi*. You can easily find them in Indian grocery stores in the spices section. They are added in a curry toward the end for aroma and an earthy taste.

Dried Red Chiles: Dehydrated red chiles are often used in Indian cuisine to flavor the food and add color. Kashmiri red chiles are used primarily for their bright color and milder taste. You can replace them with locally available mildly hot dried red chiles.

Dahi (Curd): You can replace it with plain, thick Greek yogurt. Make sure to whisk dahi or yogurt until smooth and lump free before adding it to the curry.

Curry Leaves: This is an aromatic herb mainly used for seasoning curries. Do not confuse curry leaves with curry powder.

Cooking Oil: I have used mainly ghee, mustard oil and coconut oil to cook a variety of curries. Both mustard and coconut oil are vegan ingredients. You can replace ghee with unsalted butter, and mustard oil with sunflower, groundnut or peanut oil.

Coconut: In many recipes, I have used coconut to make a curry paste. You can use freshly chopped, grated, desiccated or frozen coconut for the same purpose.

Coconut Milk: In each recipe, I have specified the type of coconut milk required—thick or thin. Thick coconut milk is the first-pressed milk. Both kinds have a different consistency and help to define the consistency of the curry. You can replace thick coconut milk with coconut cream.

Chicken: For a curry, the best choice would be bone-in meat pieces. The chicken bones lend a delicious flavor to the curry. You can use a combination of bone-in chicken thigh and the leg piece. If you are using boneless chicken breast pieces, then try not to use frozen ones.

Cream: In India, we use light cream with 25 percent fat for cooking. But any cooking cream works for these curry recipes.

Ginger and Garlic Paste: A smooth paste of ginger and garlic is one of the most common Indian ingredients. You can use jarred ginger and garlic paste, or blend the two ingredients in a 1:1 ratio using 1 to 2 tablespoons (15 to 30 ml) of vegetable oil or water at home. Store in the refrigerator for up to 30 days, making sure to use a clean and dry spoon each time you scoop out some paste. You can also freeze it in ice trays for up to 6 months.

Green Chiles: You can use any variety of mild to medium-hot green chiles for flavoring the curries. These include jalapeño, Thai green chile and serrano peppers. Discard the seeds of any chile to make the dish less hot.

Glass Lid: A lid comes in handy while sautéing a masala or simmering a curry to prevent splattering.

Shallots: These are related to onions, or as we call them here, sambar onion. They have a distinctive taste and add a lot of depth to the flavor of a curry.

Tempering (Tadka): *Tadka* is the Hindi term for "tempering." In a lot of Indian dishes, a tadka is added before serving the dish as a glaze or a finishing touch. It is nothing but hot ghee flavored with spices, chiles, onion, garlic or other ingredients of choice. The tadka adds an extra layer of flavor and aroma to the dish.

Acknowledgments

A heap of gratitude to my mother, who helped me become a strong, willful woman. Her delicious food and motherly guidance in the kitchen enabled me to embrace cooking as a skill early. And today, with great pride, I can say that I am what my mother made me!

While my mother instilled the love for food in me, my husband gave me the courage and wings to follow my dreams. He helps me become a better version of myself. They say, "Behind every successful man, there is a woman." For me, he is the force behind my success and the official food taster of this cookbook.

We all need great cheerleaders to sail through the highs and lows of life; mine came in a furry package of four-legged cuteness, called Momo—the pug—a food connoisseur, a chicken lover and my constant source of positivity. Unfortunately, he won't be with me on the release date as he left this earth for a better place before I could finish this book. But he will always be my constant source of positivity. And then I am blessed with a big family of loving in-laws, a brother and aunts, who help me stay connected with my cultural roots and are always happy to share their secret recipes.

But this book couldn't have happened without my editor, Tamara, who trusted in my ability to write a cookbook, and Caitlin. Always so patient and calm. You two will be forever special!

And above all, a big THANK-YOU to every reader of my blog, ever-growing social media family and real friends, who for years have been a persistent part of my journey, always honest with feedback and my most incredible supporters.

About the Author

Hina Gujral is a recipe creator and the creative force behind her food blog Fun FOOD Frolic. Born and raised in India, she is among the country's top food influencers.

A former financial analyst, Hina allowed her lifelong passion for food to become her purpose and turned it into a full-time profession. She has shared her inspiring journey from banker to blogger on the TEDx platform.

Hina's philosophy is easy, everyday comfort food that feels like a warm hug and melts your heart—the kind of meals she grew up eating. Her intercultural marriage into a Sikh family of food lovers, as well as her extensive travels across the country and hours of labor in the kitchen, has given her unmatched first-hand experience cooking Indian food. She understands the nuances of Indian cuisine, and the 100 recipes in this cookbook are the best example of her culinary skills.

INDEX